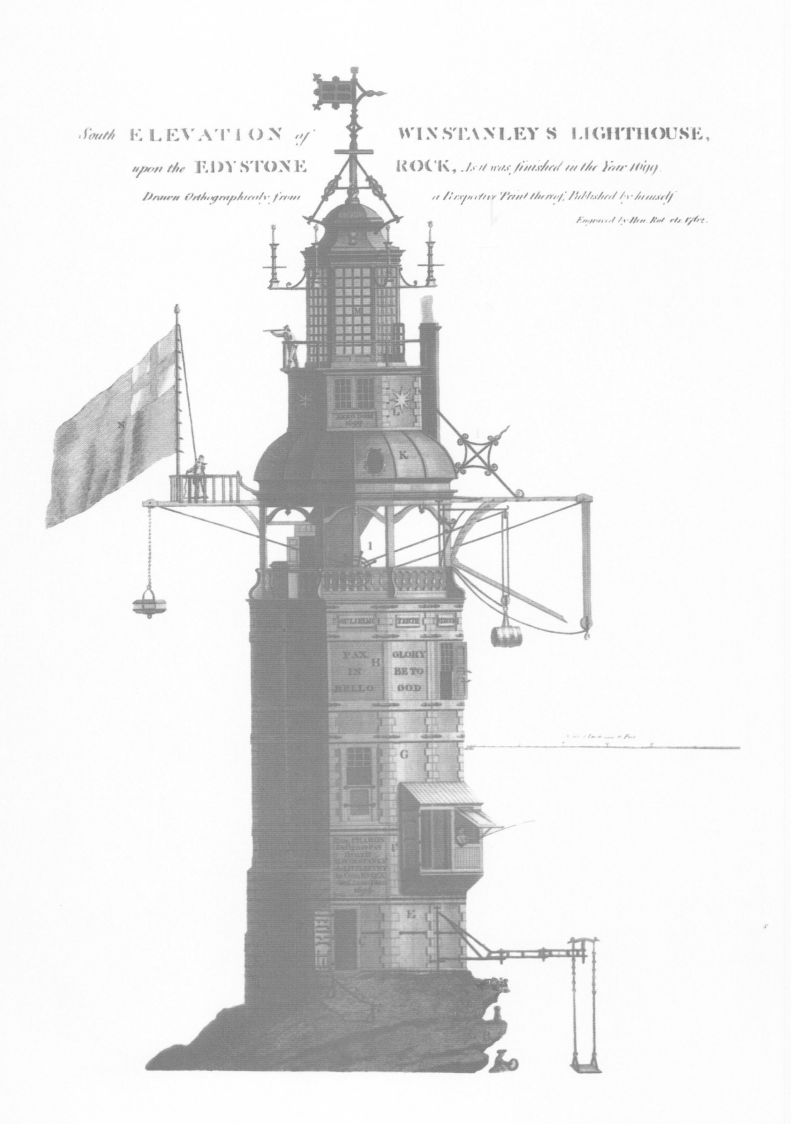

South ELEVATION of WINSTANLEY'S LIGHTHOUSE, upon the EDYSTONE ROCK, As it was finished in the Year 1699. Drawn Orthographicaly from a Perspective Print thereof, Published by himself

Engraved by Hen. Roberts 1762.

BEACON ON THE ROCK

*the dramatic history of lighthouses
from Ancient Greece to the present day*

PETER WILLIAMS

AURUM PRESS

A QUINTET BOOK

First published in Great Britain by
Aurum Press Ltd
25 Bedford Avenue
London WC1B 3AT

A catalogue record for this book is available from the British
Library

ISBN 1 85410 817 4

10 9 8 7 6 5 4 3 2 1
2005 2004 2003 2002 2001

This book was designed and produced by:
Quintet Publishing Limited
6 Blundell Street
London N7 9BH

Senior Project Editor: Laura Price
Editor: Andrew Armitage

Designer: Isobel Gillian
Picture Researcher: Helen Stallion
Illustrator: Richard Burgess

Creative Director: Richard Dewing
Editorial Director: Jeremy Harwood

Publisher: Oliver Salzmann

Manufactured in Hong Kong by Regent Publishing Services Ltd.
Printed in China by Lee-Fung Asco, Printers Ltd.

PICTURE CREDITS

AKG: 13; Alec Waugh: 34 (bottom); Bernard Gribble: 126 (bottom); Bob
Strickland S.W.C.D.A.: 187 (top and insets); Britten: 29, 30 (top), 31, 48,
70 (bottom), 71, 92 (bottom), 109, 146 (top), 158, 168 (left), 169, 179
(right); Bruce Roberts: 45, 50 (bottom), 72 (top), 75 (right), 86-87, 117
(bottom), 148-9 (middle), 162-3, 178 (bottom), 180 (left), 181 (top), 184
(top),185 (all), 191; Chris Mills: 64 (bottom), 94 (top), 176 (top), 183
(right); 173; Corbis: 36 (bottom), 39 (bottom), 41, 61, 151 (top), 160
(bottom); David Rye 18 (bottom); Dundee Courier: 78 (top); Egbert Koch: 7
(left and right), 62 (bottom left), 154 (bottom), 130 (bottom); Fredrich-Karl
Zemke: 130 (bottom); Gert Fopma: 174 (bottom), 177; Glasgow Evening
Citizen: 116 (left and right); Gleasons Pictorial: 42 (bottom); Hague
Collection: 4, 12 (bottom); 14 (bottom), 15 (top), 16 (top and bottom), 18
(bottom), 20 (bottom left and right), 21, 32, 35 (left), 54 (top), 59 (bottom
left), 60 (top left and right), 63 (top), 76 (top), 79 (bottom), 80 (bottom), 81
(inset top), 84 (top), 85 (inset), 104 (bottom), 118 (top), 119, 121 (top), 124,
126 (top), 128 (bottom), 142 (top), 143, 149 (top), 161 (top), 165 (bottom);
Hans-Guenter Spitzer: 68; Hilary Surtees: 7 (middle), 46 (middle); Hulton
Picture Library: 11, 159 (top), 140 (bottom); Hubert Hall: 6 (left); J.A.N.A.:
31 (full); Jerry Biggs: 50 (top), 137 (bottom); Jim Dobbins: 105 (left and
right); James Hyland:147 (bottom), 150 (bottom); Joan Huyland: 89; Joanne
Bond: 102 (top); John Eagle: 51 (right); John Hellowell: 1, 6 (left), 64 (top);
John Hyland: 131 (top); John Mobbs: 51 (middle), 53 (left), 72 (bottom);
Juergen Tronicke: 19 (right); K. Sutton-Jones: 56 (top right and left), 58
(bottom left); Karl Spitzer: 115 (bottom), 189 (bottom); Kjell Otto Hansen:
115 (top left); La Trobe Library, Coppin Collection via Donald Walker: 35
(right); Lionel Derek Scott BEM: 110 (bottom); Lord Greenway: 124 (top);
Mark Stansfield: 137 (middle); National Maritime Museum: 120 (bottom);
Northern Lighthouse Board: 155 (top left and right); Peter Williams
Collection: 10, 22 (top), 47 (bottom), 51 (left), 52 (right), 53 (right), 61
(insets), 62 (bottom right), 82 (top), 91 (top), 96 (bottom), 98 (bottom), 106
(top), 122 (top), 123, 132 (bottom), 138, 139, 144, 145, 148 (left),
166 (top), 166 (bottom right), 182 (top), 182 (bottom), 189 (top), 132
(bottom); 134 (top), 136 (inset), 141 (top), 156 (top), 168 (right); Philip
Simons: 47 (top); Plisson: 2-3, 23, 37, 55, 70 (top), 77, 83 (bottom), 85, 99,
101, 103, 107, 108 (bottom), 111, 112-113, 115 (top right), 127 (top), 152-
153, 157, 164 (left), 170 (left), 171 (top), 188 (bottom); Plymouth Museum
and Art Gallery: 27 (bottom); Ralph B.Starr (U.S.L.H.S.): 125 (bottom);
R.N.L.I.: 97 (box); R.I.B.A.: 26; Saison: 93 (top); Saturday Evening Post: 95;
Science and Society Library: 25 (top left and right), 57, 59 (top right), 62
(top), 66 (bottom), 67, 73 (right), 80 (top), 81 (bottom), 81 (inset bottom),
83 (top), 88 (top); Schiffahrt: 134 (bottom); Tideland: 166 (bottom left);
Tom Tag: 58 (bottom right); Trinity House: 24 (bottom), 69 (top), 100
(bottom), 122 (bottom), 129, 133 (right), 135 (top), 136 (full page), 167,
172; U.S.C.G. National Archives: 43 (top and right), 125 (top); U.S. Library
of Congress: 28 (bottom); 42 (top); Wayne Wheeler U.S.L.S.: 44 (bottom);
Western Telegraph: 65 (top); World Ships:137 (top).

Author's Acknowledgement:
The author wishes to thank the worldwide band of lighthouse engineers,
attendants and enthusiasts, and contributors to his lighthouse journal,
Leading Lights, who have assisted, sometimes unwittingly, in this book by
sharing with him their knowledge and enthusiasm for lighthouses and light
vessels. To select names would be invidious; they know who they are and that
any mistakes they find are my responsibility.
Peter Williams

CONTENTS

INTRODUCTION

Lighthouses have a special place in the heart of mankind. These often majestic structures have saved many human lives — as well as valuable cargoes — from watery graves on inhospitable coastlines all over the world. The lighthouse keepers played their part, too, as we shall see, with many acts of individual heroism when succoring the shipwrecked, sometimes surrendering their own lives in the attempt.

The lighthouse is an icon of rugged reliability, probably more so than any other structure built by mankind. Lighthouses have been beacons, homes, and refuges, and today remain symbolic of the world's maritime heritage.

This book is a voyage of exploration that starts by looking at the early primitive beacons. Some were no more than open fires on exposed headlands; others, as we shall see in the case of the Pharos at Alexandria, were magnificent structures. But, whether simple fires or tall towers, they guided the mariner into his safe haven. Like the ships that they served, the development and design of lighthouses was slowly but continually improved—as was the equipment they used to provide the light. The men responsible for this development came from a wide variety of backgrounds: some, such as Henry Winstanley, who built the first offshore lighthouse on the Eddystone Rock off the south of England, were well-known merchants of their time; others rose from relatively obscure, even humble, beginnings to make a name for themselves. Others were in it just for the money!

North American shores were lit almost as soon as they were colonized, and our exploration will show how the colonists built lighthouses by following European methods—and in some cases even importing materials and lamps from the Old World.

Our voyage will continue by looking at the improvement of lamps from the simple oil-pot lamp to the modern solar-generated electric light source. We will see how the simple fixed light evolved into a multi-beamed, flashing, coded light that enabled the navigator to know exactly which lighthouse the vessel was passing.

During the period covered by this book, many different fuels for the lamps were tried, and some, such as kerosene, were adopted worldwide and used for decades. Others, such as the oil from sheep's tails used in South African lighthouses, or that extracted from porpoises at Cape Hatteras Lighthouse off North Carolina, had limited success. And no lighthouse history would be complete without mention of the range of sound signaling devices used in place of the lamp during fog.

Though modern lighthouses are now operated automatically—which is the subject of an entire chapter— we will also look in depth at the lives of some of the people who built and operated them. Some of the stories that unfold here have an element of drama, some have humor, but almost all show the dedication of the those involved in fighting the elements to keep a light shining. Family life is not forgotten: even the grandest civil engineer, while away from home building his latest lighthouse, had left behind a family who would worry about his safety. The keepers, on the other hand, had their families with them, sharing the lonely lifestyle, assisting with the light, and sometimes, sadly, taking over the duty on the sudden demise of the keeper through sickness or accident.

Often forgotten—because they are not normally in the public eye—are the lightships off the coast. Moored on shoals at the mercy of wind and tide, they have mostly been replaced by buoys or lighthouses. Those that remain on station have been converted to unmanned operation. Their decks will never again be a place of danger for the crew during storms, or in less hazardous moments be an envied fishing spot on a calm summer's afternoon. The trials and tribulations of these very special ships and crews are documented in these pages to serve as a reminder to all of us of a way of life that is gone and highly unlikely to return.

The move toward automation and the remote control of lighthouses has meant that almost all lighthouse keepers have now been made redundant. Lighthouses are now visited by technicians to correct faults or carry out planned maintenance. The very need for lighthouses has been questioned with the advent of satellite-derived global positioning equipment. And so, the final chapter in our voyage will show how the preservation and conservation of our world's stock of lighthouses is being undertaken.

Some lighthouses, whether redundant or still in use as aids to navigation, are being given additional or alternative use as museums, homes, and visitor attractions. Whatever the modern role, they remain fascinating glimpses of our maritime past.

Chapter 1 | THE EARLIEST BEACONS

Since humanity first sought to conquer the sea, it has needed markers to help guide the way.
Today, we know these markers as lighthouses and lightships. However, seamarks — as they are more
generally known — have not always been the idealized vision of a tall, cylindrical building
with a light in the top.

THE FIRST SEAMARKS USED BY developing civilizations in ancient times were natural phenomena, landmarks, and fires used as homing beacons. Some seamarks were probably statues and other prominent shore objects rather than dedicated lighthouses. Indeed, one of the Seven Wonders of the World, the Colossus of Rhodes, which legend suggests was at the entrance to the main harbor on the Greek island from which it takes its name, has been claimed, though without justification, to be the earliest lighthouse. It was, if we believe the legend, a statue of a warrior of immense proportions whose legs straddled the harbor entrance. One tale has it that the upraised hand held a beacon flame, while another suggests that the eyes lit up like glowing coals.

The Pharos at Alexandria—another of the Seven Wonders—is widely accepted as the first major lighthouse in the world. Julius Caesar (100–44 B.C.E.) described it as being "of great height and wonderful construction;" the Greek geographer and historian Strabo (63 B.C.E. to C.E. 24) wrote in his book *Geography*: "… it was built of white marble." The lighthouse was named after the island at the entrance to Alexandria, one of the main trading ports in the Greco-Roman world.

The Greek architect Sostratus of Cnidos was responsible for the design, which he undertook for the Egyptian king Ptolemy I (c. 367–283 B.C.E.). The king authorized the building in 290 B.C.E. and it was completed 20 years later at great cost. Ptolemy did not live to see the light exhibited. When Sostratus wished to carve his own name on the lighthouse, Ptolemy's son, Ptolemy II (309–246 B.C.E.), refused. He commanded that only the word "Ptolemy" be inscribed. This annoyed Sostratus, who resorted to a clever act of guile to get his own way: he had an inscription bearing his name chiseled into the stonework. This was plastered over and the word "Ptolemy" was cut into it. Sostratus knew that weathering would wear this away and expose his name forever. Sostratus's inscription read: "Sostratus son of Dexiphanes of Knidos on behalf of all mariners to the savior gods."

Research in 1904 by a German historian, Herman Thiersch, indicates that the tower was built as a stepped pyramid starting from a base 350 feet (about 107 meters)

RIGHT *Medieval painting of the early lighthouse at Boulogne showing the spiralling outer and highlighting the impressive impact of the structure on the skyline.*

square. The tower rose over 400 feet (122 meters) with a further tower—a smaller, round construction—holding a fire basket on the top of the main structure. Some descriptions do not agree with this and say that the fires were in closed chambers open only toward the sea. A staircase spiraled up to allow wood to be carried up for the fire. The fire would have burned with as much smoke as flame, making a better mark by day than night.

Even by modern standards, the amount of light put out by this ancient structure was impressive. The Jewish historian Flavius Josephus (C.E. 37 or 38–c. 101) recorded that the range of the light was 300 stadia (about 29 nautical miles or 33 land miles). The amount of fuel needed must have been many tons—maybe even 5 or 6 tons a night to keep such a huge flame going—each bundle being carried by slaves up the spiral stairway in an unending procession. The keeper's role was often more that of a slavemaster than that of a lighthouse attendant.

This magnificent light remained in place for over 1,500 years, suffering the effects of many land tremors before an earthquake finally destroyed it in the fourteenth century.

A French archaeological expedition was mounted in 1994 at the request of the Egyptian government. The divers found some artifacts and large stone blocks that they thought were some parts of the lighthouse that were covered when the fort at Qaitbey was built in the 1480s on the site of the ancient lighthouse. The present Alexandria Lighthouse is a 180-foot-high (55 meter) white tower that was constructed by the French in 1848 at Ras el Tin and is still in operation.

The Pharos gave its name not only to pharology, the study of lighthouses, but is also the root of the word for lighthouses in many languages: *phare* in French, *faro* in Italian and Spanish, and *farol* in Portuguese.

The Roman Empire built up a network of routes by land and sea. These routes allowed rapid communication between the Roman emperors and their provincial governors. They were also used for the movement of troops to subjugate the less civilized lands. The Romans left behind roads and lighthouses, some so well planned and constructed that, though ruins, they remain to the present day. Huge stone towers were built with open fire baskets, known as cressets, on the top. Details of some of these lighthouses have made fascinating subjects for mosaics, decorations on funeral urns, and engravings on coins and medals, giving historians a reasonable idea of the style of a Roman lighthouse so they can complete the picture from the ruins that remain.

One of these structures has survived at Dover in Kent in southeastern England—the Roman gateway to the country, since it is the closest town on the British mainland to Continental Europe. The colonizing Romans built two lighthouses at Dubris, as they called what we

BELOW *Lighthouses were the subjects of mosaics, coins, and medals, and so their images have been preserved to enable future generations to understand the design of early structures that no longer exist. The lower medal, struck by the Roman Emperor Commodus (161–92 C.E.), shows the lighthouse at Boulogne. The mosaic is at Ostia near Rome.*

now know as Dover. Only foundations are left to show where the light on the western heights was situated. But, in the grounds of Dover Castle, there remains the other— an octagonal stone tower that is the tallest example of Roman building in Britain.

Although the tower is only 40 feet high (12 meters), its light was exhibited 380 feet (115 meters) above the sea because of the tower's position. It would have been visible from the tower at Tour D'Ordre at Boulogne in northern France, creating not only a useful beacon but a signal station, too.

The tower was constructed using tufa (a porous, spongy-looking rock) and green sandstone, with bonding courses of red tiles. The eight levels were plank floors with access ladders to the beacon. By C.E. 500 the Romans had abandoned their colony, and Dubris Lighthouse became dark and derelict. The durable tower remained in good condition, though, enabling stonemasons in the fourteenth century to convert it to a belfry and connect it to the nave of the church of St.-Mary-in-Castro.

ABOVE *A colored copper engraving of the Pharos at Alexandria after Johann Berhard Fischer engraved by Erlach, circa 1700.*

Closer to home, another notable lighthouse was built in C.E. 50 at Ostia, southwest of Rome, which was the city's chief port. The lighthouse is even depicted in a mosaic, a pavement that was uncovered in the ruins of Ostia in the nineteenth century. It shows a solidly built, tiered, square stone tower with a cresset on the top. It was reputed to have been built on the instructions of Emperor Claudius (10 B.C.E.–C.E. 54) on the sunken hulk of a great ship that was used to transport a massive monolith from Alexandria to Rome. During excavations at Ostia in the 1950s, a Roman plan of the harbor was uncovered, as were the remains of a ship (311 by 70 feet/94.8 by 21 meters) filled with a giant stone. There were similar towers at Ravenna, Capri, and Pozzuoli (which the Romans called Puteoli) and at many other Roman ports. The lighthouse at Aegea is represented on a coin issued by Antioch IV of Syria in 175 B.C.E.

BUILT TO LAST

The Roman Tower of Hercules, the oldest working lighthouse in the world, was built on a rocky peninsular near present-day Corunna, on the northwestern coast of Spain. When constructed in C.E. 400, it was a major seamark on the trading route to the Roman provinces of Galacia and Gaul. The lighthouse—built by a Romanized native of Portugal, Gaius Sevius Lupus, about whom little else is known—is mentioned in the Mappa Mundi, a monastic scroll dating from 1285. The light was abandoned during the decline of the Roman Empire and not used again until the seventeenth century. In 1682, the beacon was re-established by the Spanish, who placed two coal-fired cressets on the ruined tower. The tower was repaired in 1791, but the cressets were not replaced with oil lamps and reflectors until the early 1800s.

The present 158-foot (48-meter) tower dates from 1847, when a Fresnel lens system (see Chapter 3) was fitted. The tower remains in use to this day, although it now employs an electric lamp. The change to electric power came in 1926, when the lighting equipment was modernized by the French lighthouse engineers Barbier, Bernard, and Turenne.

BELOW *The Roman lighthouse at Boulogne, known as the Tour d'Ordre, as drawn in 1549.*

The collapse of the Roman Empire left not only the lighthouse at Corunna extinguished, but many others, too, including those at Ostia and Dover. Another was a tower built by Caligua (C.E. 12–41) at Boulogne in northern France, known as the Tour d'Ordre, in C.E. 40 to celebrate his "triumph" over Neptune, the Roman god of the sea. It was put to more practical use as one of the beacons used by the Roman fleet undertaking the colonization of Britain. The light was on a tower 125 feet (38 meters) high; the distance between the octagonal faces at its base measures 65 feet (20 meters) with each of the 12 stages reducing in steps with height until the small open fire platform was reached. It became another victim of the decline of Roman power and may have been relit by the Holy Roman Emperor Charlemagne (742–814) in 800 C.E. The tower was destroyed in 1644. It fell into the sea when the cliff on which it was built collapsed into the waves below.

DARKER TIMES

The decline of the Roman Empire left not only the lighthouse at Corunna extinguished, but many others too. As the Romans' influence receded, lighthouses fell into disuse and disrepair. There were no major lights shown on coasts or in harbors, from the decline of the Roman Empire until the early mini-renaissance in the twelfth century. Seafarers from the Scandinavian lands dominated the period from C.E. 600 until C.E. 1100. The Vikings set out on voyages of exploration and were essentially raiders with a fierce reputation for destruction and enslavement of those unfortunate enough to be in their path. Placing lights on shore could be hazardous, so settlements tended to be hidden away from the shores.

A few lights and beacons were known from monastic manuscripts to have been placed on the coasts of England and France in the ninth century. These were no more than a candle placed in their chapel windows by the early Christian priests who had taken to living on remote islands and headlands. The monk Ninian, for example, built his dwelling in the fifth century on the headland of the Isle of Whithorn off the southwest coast of Scotland. Mariners approaching the Solway Firth used his house as a daymark (the term sailors use for an unlit but prominent landmark), but it is not known whether he exhibited a light at night. He would have almost certainly have burned a devotional candle, whose light would have guided shipping.

The general lack of lighting lasted until the twelfth century. There are no records of any permanent lights built by the Vikings during their tenure of the lands wrested from the unfortunate inhabitants. They may have built temporary beacon fires to guide in the store boats that followed the

ABOVE *Painting of the Lighthouse at Genoa by John Serres, circa 1800.*

fighting long ships. Permanent lights were not used even to light harbors, because those defending them were afraid that any lights would assist an invader. This state of affairs lasted until the re-emergence of law and order, first in the Italian city merchant states and a century later in the countries bordering the North and Baltic Seas.

Typically, the merchants of Port Pisano (Pisa) established a lighthouse in 1157 at Meloria. Even to this day, this area has shoals (or areas of shallow water) to catch the unwary shipmaster. The lighthouse had a turbulent history. It was sacked and rebuilt many times during various wars with the rival city of Genoa. Finally, in 1304, the Pisans abandoned it in favor of a more easily defended lighthouse on an isolated rock off Livorno (Leghorn). (Leonardo da Vinci recorded this lighthouse in 1500 on his highly detailed map of the Tuscany coast. This showed the positions of the principal lighthouse plus three other harbor lights.)

While the Genoese were busy destroying their enemy's lighthouses, they were also astute enough to build their own. Old city records show that the city senate were collecting dues for a lighthouse on a headland they called Capo di Fari (Lighthouse Point). Keepers lit a flare of burning straw or pitch. (One of the keepers in 1449, incidentally, was an Antonio Culumbo, the uncle of Christopher Columbus, who some 40 years later, would "discover" America.) The lighthouse was badly damaged in 1544 during one of the regular wars with the neighboring city state of Pisa. An elegant square brick tower with a much improved oil lantern was built as a replacement. The 200-foot (60-meter) structure remains the tallest brick-built lighthouse tower in the world.

As with all tall structures, lightning strikes were a problem. In medieval times this was a major fear for the superstitious keepers. Priests were frequently called upon to protect the tower and its keepers with religious ceremonies. However, over the centuries, the mysterious and terrifying forks of fire in the firmament became better understood, and science took over from superstition. Eventually, in 1780, lightning conductors, recently invented in the United States by Benjamin Franklin, were fitted, providing a low-resistance path for the discharge of energy, and so protecting the structure itself.

This successful, conspicuous Genoan lighthouse encouraged the building of more such towers throughout Europe. Many early experiments with lamps, wicks, and

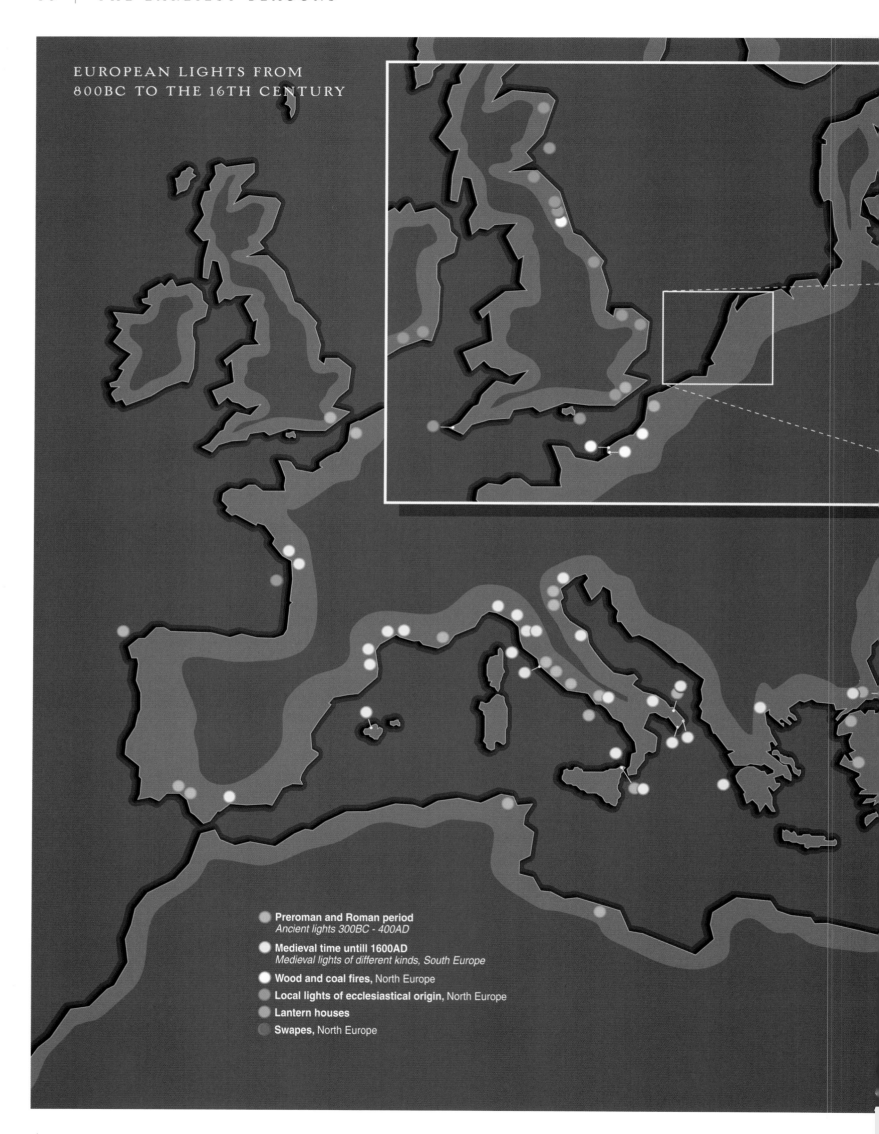

EUROPEAN LIGHTS FROM
800BC TO THE 16TH CENTURY

- Preroman and Roman period
  Ancient lights 300BC - 400AD
- Medieval time untill 1600AD
  Medieval lights of different kinds, South Europe
- Wood and coal fires, North Europe
- Local lights of ecclesiastical origin, North Europe
- Lantern houses
- Swapes, North Europe

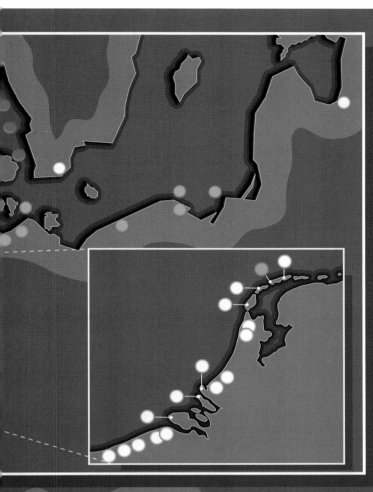

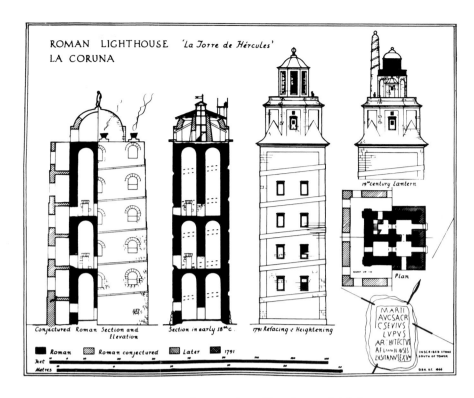

ABOVE *Cross-section of La Coruña Lighthouse*

LEFT *The chart shows the grouping of the early lights on the coast, where trading ports had been founded. Each area favored a particular type of light.*

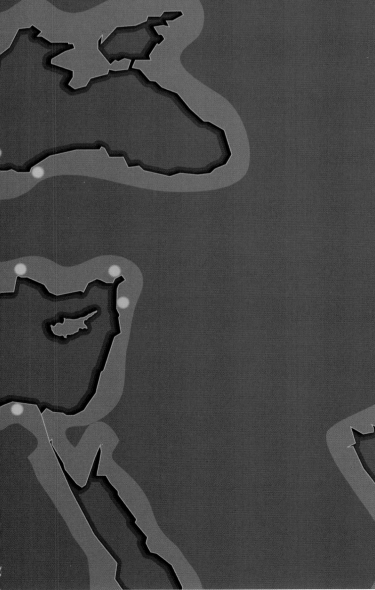

ABOVE *Aigue Mortes lighthouse, France.*

glazing were known to have been carried out here. About 30 main coastal lights and innumerable harbor lights were established, but all but one or two have vanished into obscurity. Many were, however, recorded in charters, accounts of upkeep and similar early documentation.

Most new lighthouses were of similar design to the old Roman lights, using coal cressets on simple towers with outside stairs or ladders. However, the merchants of the Hanseatic League—a federation of German communities and traders that was active from the middle of the thirteenth century to the middle of the seventeenth—used candles in hanging-lantern houses at key points on the Baltic and German North Sea coastline. Some 15 of these lights existed, and although no example has survived, although a German woodblock dated 1572 pictures one that was at Warnemunde.

The Danes, who controlled the Baltic approach from the North Sea, also provided lights, most of which were known as "swape lights." These were a flaming tar barrel on a long arm that was swung upward from ground level after lighting. It was probably more dangerous to the keeper than of use to the navigator! An example of this type of light can still be seen in the grounds of the Skagen Light at Jutland in Northern Denmark.

LISTING THE LIGHTS

After 1500, details of lights began to appear in pilotage directions and on the early sea charts. The lights were mainly ecclesiastical lights, endowed by rich people and tended by monks or hermits. One well documented example is the lighthouse operated by the monks at Hook Head in County Wexford on the southeast coast of Ireland in the thirteenth century. That this lighthouse is still in existence at all is remarkable, but the reason for is existence is even more so. It is one of the earliest examples of medieval town planning. A Norman lord, William Marshall, was developing the port of New Ross, which lies about 18 miles up the Barrow estuary from the Irish Sea. His new port depended on the ability of ships to weather the wild, low-lying Hook Head at the river entrance, so he paid for a tower to be erected on the promontory as a

BELOW *Scandinavian lights were either swape lights on headlands—our photograph shows the reconstructed light at Skagen, Jutland—or harbor lights, which, as these woodcuts from German Hansa ports show, were hanging lanterns suspended from small towers. ('Hansa' is another word for the Hanseatic League, a trading network of towns in northern Europe from the fifteenth to the sixteenth centuries.)*

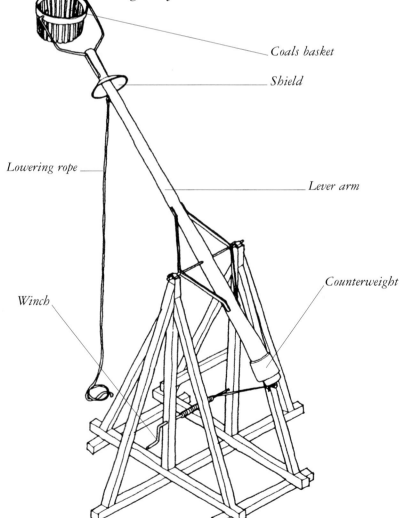

Coals basket

Shield

Lowering rope

Lever arm

Winch

Counterweight

daymark in the hours of light and fire tower at night. Estate records show that he paid the monks of St. Savior at Rendeuan (Hook Head) to build and maintain it, though he financed the maintenance by allowing the monks to extract "light dues" from ships using the harbor.

Locally quarried limestone had been used to construct a tower 82 feet (25 meters) high and 40 feet (12 meters) in diameter. The walls are 11 feet (3.5 meters) thick at ground level, tapering to about 9 feet (2.7 meters) on the two upper stories. The cells for the monks were built into the walls, as was the stairway spiraling up to the fire platform.

The light was tended by the Augustinian Order for over 400 years until their order was disbanded. Spasmodic attempts to keep it alight were made by local people after that, but the light was eventually allowed to go out.

However, the tower was in use again during the latter part of the seventeenth century after Sir Robert Reading, an Irish member of parliament, was granted a patent (then a conferring of rights rather than the protection of an invention) by the English king, William III to improve the light. He built a lantern house to enclose the fire basket. The patent allowed him to collect dues from passing ships, but it was found that his agents in Liverpool and Chester were exceeding their remit and overcharging. His patent was surrendered to the crown on November 22, 1704, and the control of the light was taken up by the commissioners appointed by the British government. A surveyor's report made to them about the light in the same year suggested that the sum of £87 10s should be spent to improve the wooden lantern house, and at the same time provide for better-quality coal, but nothing seems to have been done until much later.

Indeed, it was not until 1791 that a larger lantern containing 12 oil lamps replaced the coal grate. The platform used first by the monks and later by Reading now forms the base of the smaller tower added by the commissioners known as the Dublin Ballast Board in 1823. This addition cost £4,280 and was a great improvement. (In 1867 the operation of all lighthouses in Ireland was placed under the control of the newly formed Commissioners of Irish Lights. Systems were put in place to train lighthouse keepers and national standards of service were introduced.) Hook Head was manned by a team of keepers living on the site with their families in houses erected next to the old tower. The keepers were withdrawn in 1996 when the light was automated.

RIGHT *The lighthouse at Hook Head, still in operation in 2001, complete with rooftop radar scanner.*

PENANCE TO THE POPE

Another lighthouse looked after by a monk or hermit was built on St. Catherine's Down on the Isle of Wight in the English Channel for an entirely different reason. It was built as the result of a Papal Bull—an edict from the Pope—threatening a local squire, Henry de Godetun, with excommunication from the Catholic Church. His crime was the alleged purchase of a cargo of monastic wine that was shipwrecked off the coast of the island while being shipped from Picardy to England. The crew scrambled ashore but when the weather improved they returned to the wreck, removed the cargo and sold it to the islanders. The squire was ordered to build the lighthouse and an oratory as a penance. He also had to provide an endowment for its upkeep in perpetuity. The light was placed too high above the sea and would have been frequently obscured by fog and mist. No records exist to tell us the history of this light, though the tower was still standing in 1566. The endowment would have been swept away with the Reformation early that century.

Monastic wine, princes, and merchants were the medieval key to the founding of many lights and there are many similar stories to the one at St. Catherine's. Most endowed lights were small ones, allied to simple hermit chapels; some are documented, but most are legend.

LEFT *The lighthouse proposed by Lewis Morris, of whom little is known, for Grassholm Island off the Welsh coast in 1748. The lighthouse was never built, but the drawing clearly shows the layout of an early open-fire lighthouse.*

ABOVE *This artist's interpretation of the Dungeness Lighthouse, Kent, England, clearly shows the open fire and the fuel hoist for recharging it. The keeper's dwelling in the base of the tower must have provided dirty, cramped quarters.*

RIGHT *Henry de Godetun's lighthouse at Chale Down, St Catherine's, Isle of Wight—sometimes confused with St. Catherine's Lighthouse.*

A Lighthouse on an Island or Head=land, to direct Ships in the Night A. the Grate B. the Lightman stirring the Fire. C. a Crane to land the Coals.

ABOVE *The cresset at Flamborough Head, England.*

THE MIGHTY CORDOUAN

The great ornate lighthouse at Cordouan is still operational at the entrance to the River Gironde on the French Biscay coast. It dates from 1612, but the need for a warning there was perceived as far back as 800, when, it is said, Emperor Charlemagne placed the first light on a bare islet in the river entrance to prevent his ships coming to grief on the shifting sandbanks and swirling currents. It almost certainly fell into disuse quite soon afterwards. The next notable to light the estuary was the Edward the Black Prince (1330–76). A charter dated 1409 also tells us that he erected a chapel and tower in 1370. He paid for its upkeep by extracting dues from the Bordeaux wine shippers. The cost of repairing continual storm damage led the prince to double the dues paid by the Bordeaux merchants. He ordered the money to be paid to the incumbent keeper, a priest called de Laparre. This light was in service until 1612; it was shown on early charts as one of the principal European navigation marks.

LIGHTING ENGLAND

Lighthouses on the English coast were almost unknown before 1600. One at Tynemouth on the northeast coast is known to have existed, looked after by the monks of the nearby priory. At North Shields, not far away, two towers were built in 1540 by the shipping guild Trinity House at Newcastle. (This was a body quite independent of Trinity House itself, as were a number of other guilds that went under the name of Trinity House.) These lighthouses were the first to be chartered by Henry VIII, who also gave a

charter to Trinity House at Deptford Strond, London, in 1514, so founding an institution whose name and ideas about lighthouse administration were to become synonymous with good lighthouse practice throughout the world. The Elder Brethren of Trinity House, however, would not become enthusiastic about building and operating lighthouses for another 300 years. They relied on patents granted to private individuals who built lights not for philanthropic reasons, but as sources of income. This quaint conception gave rise to lighthouses being built in inappropriate places by people not well versed enough in the needs of the mariner. There were glaring failures and outstanding successes.

All the early lights marked landfalls, harbors, or dangerous headlands. The thought that offshore hazards should be marked either was not accepted, or, if it was, was dismissed as an impossible concept. Yet isolated shoals, reefs, and rocks claimed many ships. Their failure to arrive at their destination was so frequent an occurrence that hapless ship owners and the families of the ship's crews accepted it almost without question. One ship owner, Henry Winstanley, became exasperated after he had lost three valuable cargoes on the Eddystone reef off Plymouth, southwest England. These isolated groups of jagged rocks in the English Channel were right in the track of homeward-bound ships making for London and south coast ports. With the sandbanks of Goodwin Sands near the southeastern coast of Kent at the other end of the Channel, these reefs were considered to be the most dangerous in the world at the end of the seventeenth century. Trinity House, when petitioned in 1655, had commented that "it [marking of offshore hazards] could hardly be accomplished," though they went on to agree that a lighthouse would be desirable. In 1694 they obtained a patent from William III to erect a lighthouse.

Captain Whitfield was known to be interested in building a lighthouse on the reef, so he was contracted to undertake the work, but gave up after a preliminary survey and vanished from the scene. Winstanley was determined to place a lighthouse there, even though the reef itself would be visible only at low tide, restricting the amount of work that could be done until the building had grown to above high water level. He was not an engineer but knew about building materials as a result of having rebuilt his palatial country house. He also had an inquiring mind and an eccentric ability to construct mechanical contraptions and follies. This was to help considerably when he finally convinced Trinity House that he was the right person to put a light on the Eddystone.

RIGHT *Cordouan lighthouse, with the encircling protective seawall clearly visible at low tide.*

TRINITY HOUSE

The origins of Trinity House date from the formation of four separate Societies of Mariners, known as Trinity Houses, at Deptford and Dover in the south of England, and at Newcastle and Hull in the northeast. Why the name Trinity House was given to these societies is not known, but the first use appears to be with reference to an alms house of that name, which was at Hull.

As a national body, Trinity House was constituted in 1514, and given a royal charter by Henry VIII in that year. Its purpose is to ensure safe navigation around the coasts of the British Isles. Under the Seamarks Act of 1566, Trinity House was empowered by Elizabeth I to erect seamarks. When the Lord High Admiral surrendered his rights of beaconage, buoyage, and ballastage, he recommended that they be granted to Trinity House—and this was adopted. It was not until 1836 that Trinity House received powers to assume responsibility for the operation of all lights.

Trinity House was also given powers under the 1514 charter to regulate pilotage on the River Thames—leading eventually to the organization's acting as the Pilotage Authority for London and more than 40 other districts. Responsibility for pilotage in the districts was transferred to the various port and harbor authorities in 1988, although deep-sea pilots are still licensed by Trinity House. The body's responsibilities for aids to navigation are now discharged by the General Lighthouse Authorities of the United Kingdom and the Republic of Ireland, which comprises Trinity House, the Commissioners of Irish Lights, and the Northern Lighthouse Board. Trinity House has responsibility for 72 lighthouses and 11 lightships, as well as buoys, beacons, and radio-navigation systems. It also has charitable functions, providing support for young people seeking careers as officers in the merchant navy and sheltered accommodation for retired seafarers.

Trinity House's governing body is known as the Elder Brethren. Its members are drawn from the Younger Brethren, who are all either ships' masters or naval officers who are navigation specialists. You become one of the Younger Brethren because of the nature of your work, and are invited to join by existing members.

As soon as he had signed the contract in June 1696, Winstanley organized boats and a workforce in nearby Plymouth and started work, drilling holes for the iron securing rods on the highest point of the rocks. Autumn gales and winter weather stopped work, but his masons resumed the next summer, fixing the rods and building a base for the tower.

The work suffered a further setback when a French privateer captured Winstanley and his men during June 1697. Normally, the navy provided a guard ship to protect the site from depredations by the French, pirates, or thieves. On the day that the workmen were captured the naval guard ship had slipped its moorings to chase and capture the rich prize of a French merchant ship. The privateer took the opportunity to raid the unguarded workings. They set the workmen adrift in open boats but considered that Winstanley was worth a profitable ransom and took him to France, where he was imprisoned. The French king, Louis XIV, on hearing of the incident, declared that he did not wage war on humanity, and that the lighthouse was of benefit to all. He immediately set Winstanley free, rebuking the privateer captain. An

ABOVE LEFT The original Eddystone lighthouse, the first light to be placed on Eddystone Rocks, 14 miles off the coast of Plymouth. built by Henry Winstanley and completed between 1696 and 1700.

ABOVE Rudyerd's Eddystone lighthouse, from an engraving dated 1703.

exchange of prisoners was quickly arranged and Winstanley returned to Plymouth and work on the lighthouse returned almost to normal, except that the construction crew returned to Plymouth each night, which delayed the operations.

In spite of storm delays and the capture of Winstanley and his men, they persevered until they had completed the tower and lit its candle chandelier on November 16, 1698. That winter the keepers advised Winstanley that storm waves had gone right over the top of the 80-foot (24-meter) tower. He decided to remove it and build a better lighthouse. This he did the following summer, increasing the original diameter by 24 feet (7 meters), and the height by another 40 feet (12 meters).

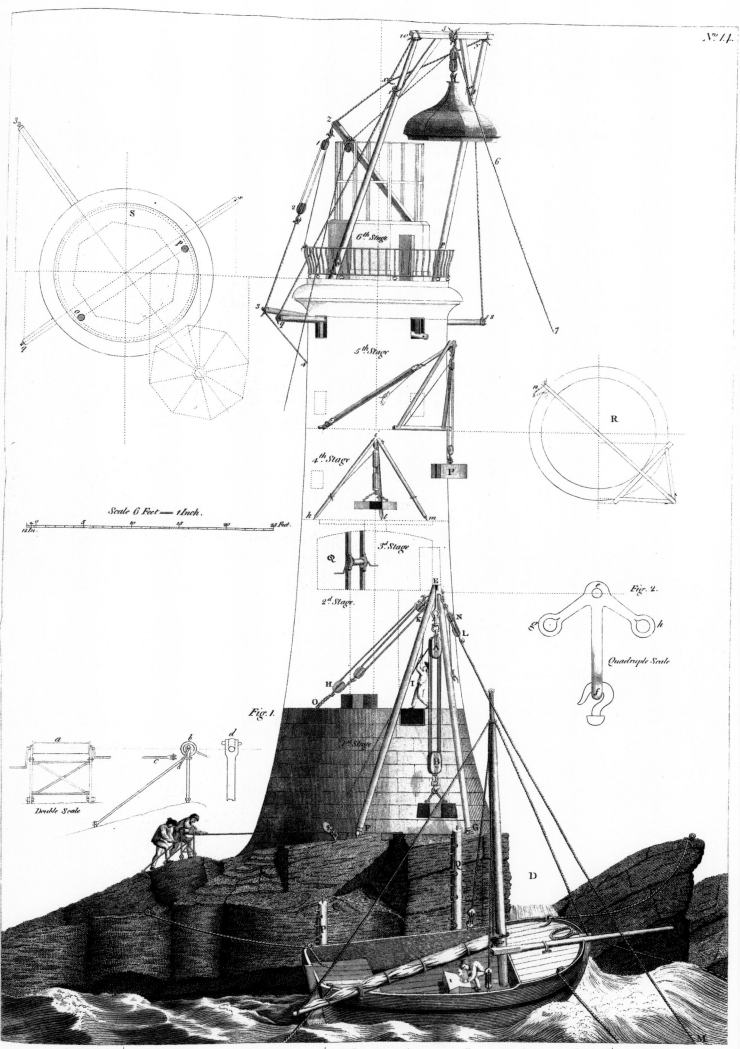

N.º 14.

6ᵗʰ Stage

5ᵗʰ Stage

4ᵗʰ Stage

3ᵈ Stage

2ᵈ Stage

Scale 6 Feet = 1 Inch.

Fig. 2.

Quadruple Scale

Fig. 1.

Double Scale

A View of the ROCK on the EAST SIDE, and of the WORK advanced to Course XV. being the first of the ENTRY COURSES,
Shewing the manner of LANDING and HOISTING the STONES &c in every Stage of the BUILDING.

The Figures by Mr C. R. Ryley.

J. Record Sculp. 1786.

The new light was shown before the turn of the year. Much to public disbelief, the new tower survived. Sadly for Winstanley, and the shipmaster who had become used to seeing its welcoming light, the lighthouse was destroyed in 1703 by some of the worst storms Britain had ever known, taking with it the builder and some of his men, who were on the tower at the time. On the morning of November 27, the stunned citizens of Plymouth noted that nothing remained of the first offshore lighthouse in the world. It was not replaced for many years.

Some three decades later, at the other end of the English Channel, a different approach was considered. In 1731, Robert Hamblin and David Avery, two London merchants, had a plan to anchor a ship, exhibiting a bright light, over a sandbank to warn ships away. His novel idea used an old flat-bottomed hulk with oil or candle lanterns hoisted to the end

LEFT *Working drawings and cross-sections of the Smeaton-designed Eddystone lighthouse.*

BELOW *Painting of the fourth Eddystone lighthouse from 1868 by William Gibbons of Plymouth.*

of her yardarm. His lightship was moored on the Nore Sand in the busy entrance to the River Thames and was financed by tolls collected from ships sailing into London to trade. The lightship was favorably commented on by shipmasters. They found that it helped them in spite of its poor light and the fact that it often drifted out of position during a storm!

LIGHTS BEGIN IN BOSTON

As the first settlers arrived on the East Coast of North America in the early part of the seventeenth century, they would have marked the landing sites and embryo harbors with a daymark, and may have used a lantern at night.

But the first lighthouse that we can be sure about was the European-style tower light erected on Little Brewster Island in the approaches to Boston Harbor in 1715–16. As with the Old World, it was the merchants who petitioned to get the light built. Boston merchants had lost a number of ships on the islets and bars that made up the entrance to their harbor. In 1715, the Court of Massachusetts (the state's legislative body) appointed a commission to look into whether there was a need to build

a lighthouse, and quickly agreed with the merchants that there was. So they recommended that one be built on the island at the entrance to the harbor. The court authorized the scheme, and, as importantly, arranged the finance. Just over one year later, on the evening of September 14, 1716, the light was exhibited. The tall graceful tower was built of stone with a conventional, glazed lantern and a candle chandelier for the light.

The first keeper was George Worthylake, whose annual salary was £50. This payment and the cost of maintenance and depreciation of the cost of the building were taken from a "light dues" fund set up by the court. The revenue was obtained by charging fees on the inward- and outward-bound cargoes of "one penny per tun." There were annual licenses for coastal traders and the fishing fleet. After America was formed, light dues were dropped. Worthylake was charged with keeping the light burning from sunset till sunrise, and maintaining the lighthouse in a clean and tidy manner. He faced the prospect of a £100 fine if he was found to be failing in his duties. He was also expected to carry out some piloting duties when not looking after his light, though the money gained from this would no doubt have been a welcome addition to his lighthouse pay. Two years after taking up his appointment, Worthylake, his wife, and one daughter were drowned when their boat capsized while returning to the island. His replacement enjoyed an increase in salary to £70 a year and was some years later made the principal Boston port pilot.

The Boston Lighthouse can also lay claim to having the first North American fog signal, in the form of a cannon placed near the base of the tower. It was fired when the fog came down in response to ship's cannons when they entered the harbor. The lighthouse suffered a setback in 1751 when a fire damaged some of its timbers. A temporary light using a ship's lantern was put in place while repairs were made. The reestablished lighthouse has parallels with the Genoan lighthouse on the Capo di Fari headland. It, too, suffered from both war and lightning strikes.

In 1775, during an occupation of the tower by the British in the early days of the American War of Independence, American soldiers raided it and carried off the lamps and the oil, firing the tower before they left. Repairs were attempted but further raids prevented their completion. When the British finally left in 1776, they blew up the structure. There was no light on the island until 1783, when the State of Massachusetts rebuilt the tower, which remains to this day. The tower suffered many lightning strikes, and in 1788 one of Benjamin Franklin's lightning conductors was fitted—but not without religious opposition amid cries that mere mortals should not attempt to thwart the hand of the Almighty, and that it was irreligious to do so!

While Boston boasted the first American lighthouse, the colonists of Georgia helped to put the New World on the early lighthouse map. General James Olgethorpe (1696–1785), the colony's founder, decided that the low-

BELOW *Drawing of America's first lighthouse at Little Brewster Island, Boston.*

RIGHT *Boston Lighthouse, the only lighthouse still manned by U.S. Coast Guards as required by Act of Congress.*

LEFT *Sandy Hook Lighthouse, U.S.A.*

ABOVE *New London Ledge Light, Connecticut, U.S.A.*

lying, indistinct coastline needed marking to assist his supply vessels to find Savannah, a port 20 miles up the coastal waterway. Shortly after his party arrived in 1733, he organized carpenters to erect a wooden tower as a daymark on the outermost island, Tybee. After many problems the 90-foot (27-meter) tower was finally erected in 1736. It has been described as a roofless tapered tower, timber-clad for the lower part and containing two levels. There are no reports of its being lit. It was destroyed by a storm in 1741, but it had served a useful purpose and money was found to replace it by March of the following year.

Some historians think that this second tower may have been lit at some time during its existence, since the new tower had a roof and stairway to the upper platform. Although there were no keepers, the tower was looked after by a local ship's pilot. This tower lasted until about 1770, and was eventually replaced by a brick construction.

LET THERE BE LIGHTS

Slowly, the American coast became lit as lighthouses were built at Nantucket (1746), Beavertail (1749), and New London (1760); and the famous Sandy Hook light was lottery-funded. Isaac Conro built this lighthouse, sometimes known as the New York lighthouse, in 1764; as a testament to his work, the tower remains in its original form to the present day. During the Revolution there was a great deal of military activity in the area around the lighthouse and its buildings, but no reports of damage—although American troops are known to have removed the lighting equipment to deny its use to the British. It was described in an account written by a journalist in 1764 as

> An Octagonal Figure having eight 8 sides, the
> diameter at the base 29 feet; and at the top of the wall,
> 15 feet. The Lanthorn is seven feet high; the
> circumference 33 feet. The whole construction of
> the Lanthorn is iron; the top covered in copper ...
> the whole from the bottom to top 103 feet.

Sandy Hook remains as the United States' oldest lighthouse still in operation.

We have seen that the very early lighthouses may have been built on regal whim, as monastic monuments, or for the financial dreams of man. Their strange structures, with poor illumination and a tendency to fall into the sea, set the scene for the next age of the lighthouse. The time was coming when man's innovative ideas and inherent skills were employed to create well-engineered structures in some of the remotest places in the world.

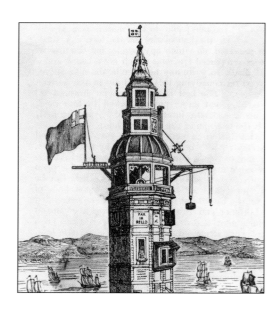

Chapter 2 | THE GUIDING LIGHT

Dr. Samuel Johnson (1709–84), the great English poet, lexicographer, essayist, and critic, defined a lighthouse as "a high tower on which to hang lanterns." His 1775 description may have been an oversimplification but essentially remains true up to today.

Most people, if asked to make a drawing of a lighthouse, would not hesitate to sketch a tapering tower with a glass lantern on the top. This description, while true of many lighthouses—especially those on offshore rocks and at the end of harbor breakwaters—does not describe the wealth of building types used to house lights.

THE DESIGN OF THE LIGHTHOUSE structure, while influenced by fashion, finance, construction materials, and the skills available to the builder, has one aim—to place a light and its equipment in a position where it is at the service of the navigator. The light has to be high enough to be visible from a distance, yet not so high to be obscured by fog and mist. The building, not always a tower, needs to be conspicuous as a landmark by day, and sturdy enough to withstand the relentless onslaught of violent weather.

Today we see such a wealth of fascinating buildings from the past and the present—buildings that house lights and their keepers are as diverse as man's inventive ingenuity. They range from the massive, stone-built offshore tower to the modern, all-glass lighthouse recently built by the Japanese at Takamatsu on northeast Shikoku in 1998. When we browse through books of pictures of famous lighthouses or buy postcards that depict them, we often fail to realize just what engineering skills, design

expertise, and brute force had to be employed to put these lifesaving beacons on the rocks of the world. Lighthouses on offshore reefs, for instance, had to have at least one characteristic in common: they needed to be massive enough not only to withstand the elements but also to support the heavy lantern and lighting equipment. Space was needed for the storage of fuel and equipment, and this was so important that finding a place for the keepers to live often seemed an afterthought! Then there was the question of the transport of materials—easier today than in the days of many of the great lighthouses of the past. For instance, there are many examples of huge lighthouses built on rocks throughout the world that have been erected far away from the source of building materials.

RIGHT *The award-winning Japanese lighthouse at Takamatsu on northeast Shikoku. Its unique construction uses a light aluminum frame and glass bricks. At night, the glass bricks are illuminated for effect.*

1849, is on the most southerly tip of South Africa. Its name means "Cape of the Needle," so called by the Portuguese because of the erratic behavior of their compass needles when off the cape, which is an area of unusual magnetic anomaly. Cape Agulhas was the last sight of land before the long haul across the Southern Ocean to the Antipodes or Asia.

This area of stormy seas between latitude 50 degrees south and the Antarctic Circle (66 south) circumscribes the earth broken only by the intrusive tip of Cape Horn. Those making for India would pass the lighthouse built on the Great Basses Reef off the southern tip of India in 1878. It was made of granite, quarried and cut into interlocking blocks at Dalbeattie, Scotland, and shipped out to the building site over 10,000 nautical miles via the stormy Cape of Good Hope. The 12–ton lantern house and lighting equipment made a similar journey from the factory of the manufacturers, Chance and Company, in the English Midlands.

RIGHT *The Great Circle route from Europe to Australia. Note how near the route is to the southern ice fields — hence, the importance of the guiding lights of the Bass Strait.*

BELOW *Cape Agulhas lighthouse on the southern tip of Africa guides ships clear of this dangerous coast.*

If heading for Australia, the light mariners would pick up would be the welcoming beam of Cape Leeuwin. This lighthouse was built on the southwestern point of Western Australia during the late 1880s. A cost-sharing agreement made between the governments of Western Australia and the eastern colonies in 1875 never materialized. This delayed the building of the lighthouse until money was made available from Western Australia's own coffers in 1885. The tower was built of local limestone on a difficult site. The contractors needed to remove tons of top cover to get to bedrock stable enough to support the 128 foot-high (39 meters) tower. The original Chance kerosene oil lamp perfected by James Timmins Chance produced a light of 250,000 candlepower; in 1925 this was changed to a pressure lamp and the output increased to 1 million candlepower. (We will explore the types of lamp in more detail in Chapter 3.)

By 1874 there were over a dozen lighthouses and lightships scattered around the shores of the New York Bay. While most North Atlantic shipping makes for U.S. ports, there are a considerable number of vessels bound for the St. Lawrence Seaway to take them into the heart of North America. They have to negotiate the fog-bound waters where the cold Labrador (or Arctic) Current meets the warm Gulf Stream.

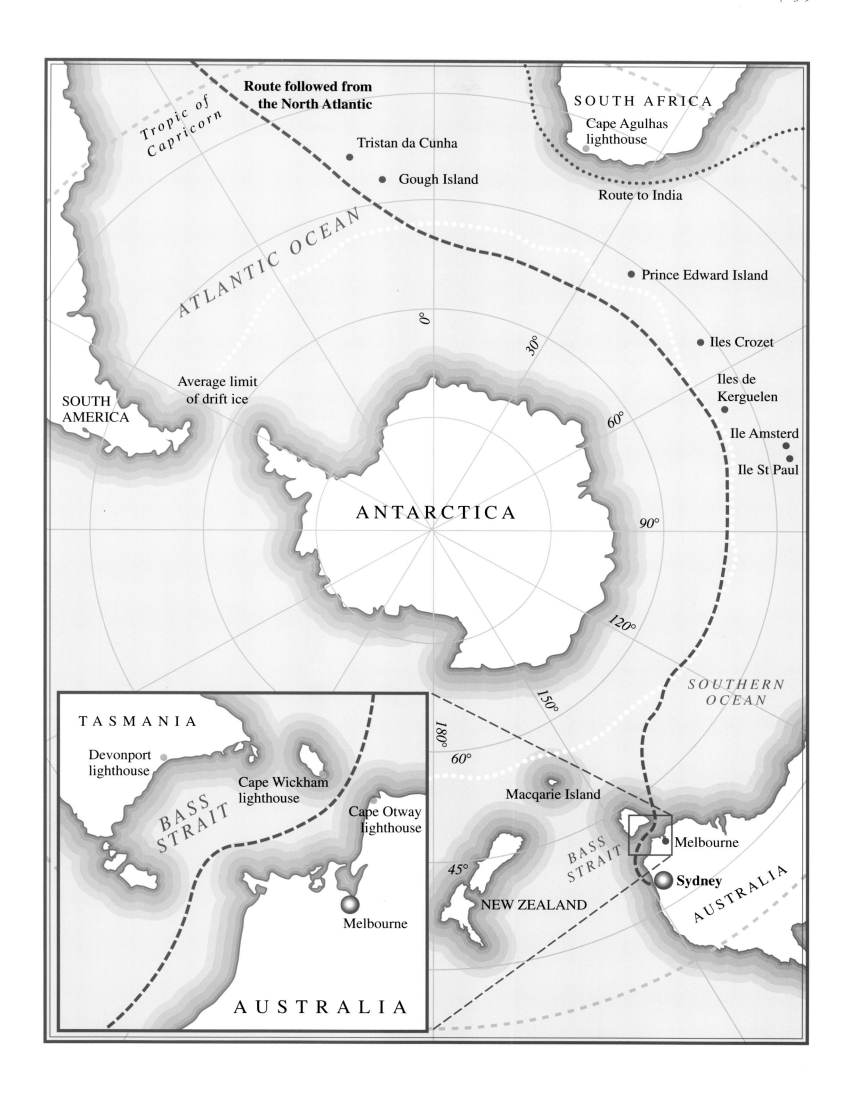

Route followed from the North Atlantic

Tropic of Capricorn

Tristan da Cunha

Gough Island

ATLANTIC OCEAN

SOUTH AFRICA

Cape Agulhas lighthouse

Route to India

Prince Edward Island

Average limit of drift ice

SOUTH AMERICA

Iles Crozet

Iles de Kerguelen

Ile Amsterd

Ile St Paul

0°

30°

60°

90°

120°

ANTARCTICA

150°

SOUTHERN OCEAN

180°

60°

TASMANIA

Devonport lighthouse

Cape Wickham lighthouse

BASS STRAIT

Cape Otway lighthouse

Melbourne

Macqarie Island

BASS STRAIT

Melbourne

45°

Sydney

NEW ZEALAND

AUSTRALIA

AUSTRALIA

The lighthouse at Cape Race, Newfoundland, is one of the key lights on the Canadian coast. The tall reinforced-concrete tower was built in 1906 to replace an earlier cast-iron tower, which had been placed on the site in 1856. Cape Race Lighthouse has a number of interesting claims to fame. The first tower was moved for reuse at Money Point at Cape Breton Island in northeastern Nova Scotia, before being moved to Ottawa, where it now stands sentinel over a main-street crossing! The tower dating from 1906 is one of the earliest reinforced-concrete structures in the world. It supports one of the largest lanterns ever made. The gunmetal and glass structure has 60 panes of glass, is 20 feet (6 meters) in diameter and 28 feet (8.5 meters) high, and weighs 24 tons. The lamp and lens assembly is one of very few hyper-radial systems still operational projecting a 1,500,000–candlepower light for 25 miles (see Chapter 3). A steam fog whistle installed in 1875 was not powerful enough and was sometimes mistaken for a ship's whistle. It was replaced by a diaphone (or two-tone) horn driven by a steam generator in 1906, giving an unmistakable bellowing sound that carried through the fog banks.

The lighthouses visited so far have all been solid structures of stone, masonry, or cast iron. Ships making the transit through the Leeward passage of the Caribbean islands use a different structure as their safe mark. The lighthouse built on Sombrero—a lonely desolate lump of rock situated 38 miles southwest of Anguilla—is one of the few lights still to be manned. It was built after a request from the British Admiralty to light the passage that had become a graveyard of ships during the middle of the nineteenth century. Disputed ownership of the islands and reluctance by the British government delayed the building until 1860.

The skeletal wrought-iron tower and its lantern were shipped out from England. The American Phosphate Company's manager looked after the new light (the company had a mining concession there) until the company abandoned the workings in 1890. Anguillan keepers were then sent to this inhospitable spot, only 40 feet (12 meters) above sea level and regularly swept by rollers even on relatively calm days. It is honeycombed with old workings and some old graves, and supports prickly cactus, black lizards, frigate birds, and terns. The area is noted for hurricanes that most seasons give the keepers some tense moments—none more so than 1898, when they reported that the winds ripped off the roof of their dwelling, causing the tower to sway alarmingly. They had difficulty standing up and were soaked by the spray that went right over the lantern. In spite of their problems, they were able to keep the light shining out. The keepers battled on. It's telling, perhaps, that a report by an inspector of the Imperial Lighthouse Service in 1930 stated that the books in their library were unread and in mint condition, even though they had been there since 1860. Either the titles were boring or they were too busy maintaining the light to find time to read them!

A steel lattice framework replaced the tower in the early 1960s. But Hurricane Donna wrecked the new structure and delayed completion by two years. In 1995 Hurricane Luis blew the windows and doors out of the south side of the dwellings, forcing the keepers to take refuge in the tower's generator room to get above the waves. The dwellings were washed clean, leaving the keepers without food and only the clothes they were wearing when the storm hit. They were out of radio contact for two days before being rescued by a Royal Navy helicopter.

FLOATING LIGHTS

Once the landfall is made there are still many hazards to overcome before a safe harbor is gained. The depths of the ocean routes are exchanged for shallower and more hazardous waters as reef, rock, and sandbank are navigated—waters that deep-sea sailors regard with horror and trepidation. Some of the busiest coastal routes are strewn with these hazards. The east coast of England is a low-lying, indistinct coastline that has shoal waters and sandbanks stretching from the notorious Goodwin Sands past the entrance to London and northward for another hundred or so miles. On shore, a chain of lighthouses, some in main streets of coastal towns, blink out their warnings. Floating lights mark the navigable channels between the banks. Some of these are now buoys, others unmanned lightships.

Until the mid-1980s the light vessels were manned by crews of 11 men operating the moored ships in all weathers. They were at the mercy of ships running them down in fog and of breaking adrift. The light vessel on the Spurn Head station suffered all these before an automatic light float replaced her in 1986. During a January gale in 1953, when the east coast was inundated by a severe storm pushing the high water right inland, the light vessel was driven off station when the anchor cable snapped. Having no engines (unlike U.S. lightships, the British vessels are towed to station), she drifted 12 miles downwind as the crew struggled to free the reserve anchors. The first one they managed to drop snagged and broke off with the force of the current. The second one held when they were in the shallow water on the Protector Shoal. They were rescued

RIGHT *The most powerful landfall light on the North American coast at Cape Race, Newfoundland.*

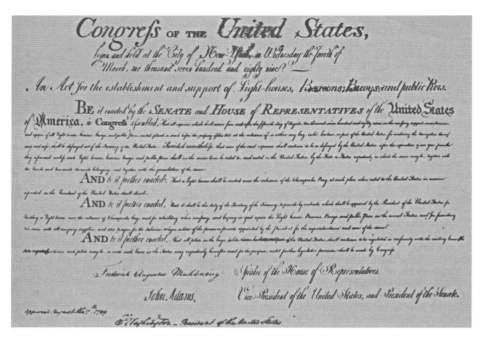

by a tug sent to chase the errant vessel. She was struck a number of times by trawlers attempting to pass too close. On one occasion she was hit amidships and rolled over by the force of the collision when a German coaster hit her in the fog. Although her light was submerged she rolled back upright. The crew were badly shaken but otherwise unhurt.

Light vessels (or lightships—the terms are interchangeable) are also used to mark wrecks or take the place of a lighthouse that's been damaged and the light extinguished. This happened in 1851 at the Cohasset Rocks off Boston on the east coast of the United States. This extensive reef is a problem for ships making for Boston and claimed many vessels. In the brief period between 1832 and 1841, 40 wrecks were recorded. The outer rock claimed many lives, one being that of a Captain Minot, who gave his name to that treacherous sweep and its subsequent lighthouses.

The story of Minot's Ledge gives an idea of the lengths that man will go to in his quest to place warning lights. This was the site of the first attempt by the U.S. Lighthouse Board (established by Congress in 1852) to build an offshore wave-swept lighthouse. Its surveyors and engineers determined that the only way to build on these rocks would be to prefabricate the components of a wrought-iron structure ashore and assemble it on the chosen site. To minimize the effect of the waves, an open pile structure (which allowed water to swirl around the

ABOVE *Minot's Ledge Lighthouse.*

RIGHT *Photograph taken in 1859 of the construction of Minot's Ledge Lighthouse to the 27th course.*

"legs," minimizing pressure from waves) was specified. The structure had had eight pillars spaced in a circle with a central pillar and cross-struts to give stability—or so it was thought.

Its stability was in doubt right from when it was first manned in 1850 until it vanished during a storm the following year. The two duty keepers were swept away. The keepers were found, one swept ashore dead, and the other still alive on one of the reefs, later dying of exposure. But the structure was lost forever. A temporary lightship was immediately placed to the seaward side of the reef, where it remained until it was replaced by a permanent vessel in 1855, built at a cost of $27,000. The 232–ton vessel remained on the station until a granite tower was built in 1860. This tower remains in service, and was manned by keepers continuously from 1850 until 1947, when automation took over. When the keepers were on duty, they lived in the top half of the 35.5 meter (114 foot) tower, its stability ensured by the way its bottom half was filled with rubble. This provided a solid enough base to counteract the pounding of the waves.

Many of the early pile lighthouses had short lives, but, as engineering expertise and the understanding of material stress and fatigue were understood, pile lighthouse construction was successfully used in coastal waters. There are examples in the African swamps. Bonny Lighthouse in the Nigerian Delta is one. The chain of pile lighthouses along the Florida Keys is another example.

Those early pile lighthouses that were sunk into sand lasted only a short time before the sea eroded the hole away and the structure was overturned by current and tide. This happened to many lighthouses, including the short-lived pile light at Brandywine Shoal in Delaware Bay, which also suffered damage from floating ice in the winter of 1828.

LIGHTHOUSE ADMINISTRATION IN AMERICA

Colonial	Federal
1716 Colony of Massachusetts built lighthouse at Little Brewster Island, Boston.	1789 Act of Congress. The fifth law of the First Congress established the lighthouse administration.
1742 Colony of Georgia built Tybee Isalnd Lighthouse.	1789 Under the control of the Secretary of Treasury.
1749 Colony of Rhode Island built Beavertail Lighthouse.	1792 Under the control of the Commissioner of Revenue.
1760 Colony of Connecticut built New London Lighthouse.	1802 Under the control of the Secretary of Treasury.
1764 Sandy Hook, New Jersey financed by New York lottery.	1813 Under the control of the Commissioner of Revenue.
1767 Colony of Delaware built Cape Henlopen Lighthouse.	1820 Under the control of the U.S. Treasury Department, 5th Auditor, Stephen Pleasanton.
1767 Colony of South Carolina built Morris Island Lighthouse, Charleston.	1837 Board of Navy Commissioners appointed.
1769 Colony of Massachusetts built lighthouse at Gurnet Point, Plymouth.	1838 Inspection of Lighthouses
1771 Colony of Massachusetts built lighthouse at Cape Ann.	1851 Board of Enquiry set up to inspect nation's lighthouse stock.
	1852 U.S. Lighthouse Board appointed.
	1903 Jurisdiction transferred to Department of Commerce.
After the War of Independence, most of the above survived and were taken over by the new federal government.	1910 Bureau of Lighthouses formed within the Department of Commerce.
	1939 Administration by U.S. Coast Guard within U.S. Treasury.

A MAJOR IMPROVEMENT

Engineering expertise came to the rescue, however. Alexander Mitchell, who was born in Belfast in Northern Ireland, invented a major improvement in pile fixing. He developed what came to be known as the "screw pile," which, just like a screw into wood, could be wound into coral or mud by a team of men using capstan bars. The screw was a split blade about 6 feet (1 meter) in diameter, which not only screwed into the seabed but also formed a bearing surface for its pile leg (once the blade was in there, with the mud above and below it, it could not move). It was a triumph over adversity, because the inventor had been blind for over 30 years when he patented his invention and started to erect lights using the method.

Mitchell first used this technique to build the lighthouse at Maplin Sands on the Thames Estuary in 1838 and followed quickly with others on mudflats on the English and Irish coasts. They were all successful and stood the test of time, and his idea soon spread to the United States. In 1840, Congress approved the money for a screw-pile lighthouse on the Brandywine Shoal. Unlike its predecessor, the Mitchell pile lasted until 1912, when corrosion of the structure rather than failure of the system led to its replacement. At Sand Key, Florida, the pile light erected in 1853 survived after hurricane-generated waves had washed away all the sandy island on which it stood, leaving the lighthouse surrounded by water. A previous conventional tower had been washed away in a similar storm.

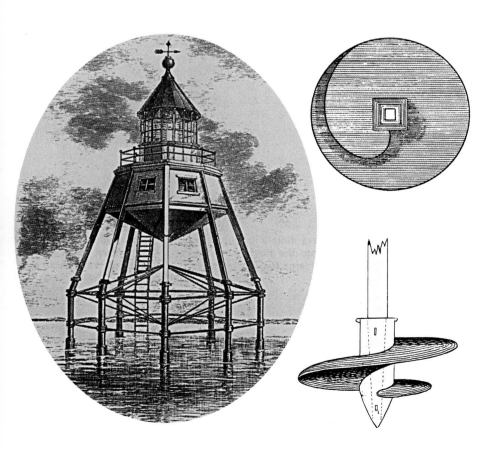

LEFT *Details of Mitchell's auger-type screw pile and a drawing of a screw-pile lighthouse.*

RIGHT *An example of a screw-pile lighthouse that was constructed at Sand Key, Florida, built in 1853 by General George Meade.*

LIGHTHOUSE ARCHITECTURE

Some early lighthouses were merely mounds of stone, just enough to hold the beacon fire in place. Others may have had architectural merit, though they have not survived for modern judgment. The few medieval structures that have survived are a tribute to their builders. However, lighthouses from the nineteenth century, the heyday of lighthouse building, have survived and are in many cases still in operation.

BELOW *A timber-built harbor light at the entrance to the River Tyne on the east coast of England. The lantern and integral oil store was favored by many harbor authorities, because it could be built by local shipwrights from easily available material. This design had the added advantage of being relatively easy to relocate if the shipping channel it lit changed course.*

LEFT *Lighthouses come in many shapes and sizes. This pier-head light at Newhaven, England, though now an electric lamp, was originally an oil lamp. Unlike lights in the U.S.A., where convention is the opposite, the red light indicates that the pier head must be to the port (left-hand) side on the way into the harbor.*

BELOW *The brick tower of the Sandy Point Shoal Lighthouse in the Upper Chesapeake Bay, Maryland, was built in 1883 on a submerged iron and concrete caisson. This strong foundation prevents damage by ice during the winter.*

NEXT PAGE *An active aid to navigation in a National Park, the Point Bonita Lighthouse, California, was built in 1877. It was the site of the first West Coast fog signal, which was a fog cannon from 1856 to 1858, when it was replaced by a bell. In 1903, the existing fog signal building was constructed, which now contains an electric klaxon. The bridge was built in 1954.*

One of the most interesting pile lights is the structure at One Fathom Bank, built in 1907 in the swirling waters of the Malacca Straits. This is one of the busiest waterways in the world, carrying traffic to and from the great port of Singapore. Mitchell's method was not used here, because the Singapore-based engineers developed a system of driving long hollow tubes through the soft seabed for 33 feet (10 meters) until they reached firm rock. To drop the piles in place, they upended them from a barge and then used water jets to burrow down through the silt. Blows finally set the piles from a 2.5–ton block of iron.

The wooden living quarters are on the lower platform and carry a framework structure that supports the service room with its $17^1/_2$-ton steel lantern house above it. The careful design and the weight of the superstructure ensured that the light is firmly held almost 100 feet (30 meters) above sea level.

The landfall, coastal, and channel-marking lights are important marks for the navigator to check that the ship is on the required course and avoiding danger. Having made a safe landfall, the ship now has to be piloted into harbor. A large ship will—and may be legally required by the harbormaster to do so—employ the assistance of a pilot with local knowledge.

For the small-craft skipper the passage in the busy and confined water of a harbor approach can be a nerve-racking experience. Whatever size of craft or amount of local knowledge available, harbor lights and leading (or range) lights will be needed in order to follow the safe channel into the quay. The prudent navigator will have consulted the chart and checked the pilotage books and lights list carried by every vessel to find the lights and marks that will act as signposts. The signposts could be just a breakwater light for the final run in, or a number of sets of leading lights as guides through the twists and turns of a long estuary.

The range lights take many different forms, from lights on skeletal beacons to wonderful and sometimes weird structures. Many in North America are keepers' homes, for example, with the lantern as part of the roof. They are always in pairs and of quite low power, but with enough intensity to outshine any shore lights. They are set so that the front light is lower than the rear one. To follow the safe course line, the shipmaster places his ship so that the higher (rear) light stays in line with the front (lower) light and steers so as to keep them so. Wandering off the line

TOP AND BOTTOM LEFT *Two example of North American lights where the lantern is part of the keeper's dwelling. Toledo Harbor Light, Lake Eerie, Ohio (top). Battery Point, California (bottom).*

THE GUIDING LIGHT | 51

will cause the apparent position of the lights to move relative to each other.

Harbor light design is as diverse as the harbors the lights are a part of, but none can be more whimsical than Metal Mickey. This iron man was made in Dublin and it was planned that he was to become a daymark on Blackrock off the coast of Sligo, Ireland. The building of a new lighthouse made him redundant before he could take up his post. Local people suggested that he be given a home in the harbor and earn his keep pointing the way to Sligo quay. He has been doing this since 1835. His brother stands on the tower on the opposite side of Ireland on Tramore daymark on the Waterford coast, it is said to remind the captains of ships to be careful navigators. There are many more stories surrounding these two unusual statues. The statue at Sligo is said to chant, "Keep off, good ship, keep off from me, for I am the Rock of Misery." And the girls of Tramore could, it was said, by hopping round their statue three times gain a husband.

But the weird and wonderful were not the only means to make lighthouses distinctive. By the turn of the twentieth century, this was achieved in the dark hours by ensuring that most lighthouses had a distinctive pattern of

BELOW, LEFT TO RIGHT *Three examples of daymarks. St Martin's daymark on the Isles of Scilly; Emmanuel Point daymark on Lindisfarne; Baltimore Beacon, Baltimore Island, Ireland.*

flashes from their lights (see in Chapter 3). But ships travel not only at night, and to be effective for the navigator lighthouses needed to be distinctive by day, too. This was achieved with the very shape of the building and, importantly, a paint scheme that would ensure that the lighthouse would show up against the background.

Where the expense of building a lighthouse is not justified, daymarks and unlit beacons are used. They range from a simple spar planted to mark an inshore shoal to a blind (lightless) lighthouse on a headland. The daymark on Gribben Head in Cornwall in the southwest of England was built in 1832 to distinguish the headland from the adjacent Dodman Point and St. Anthony's Head. It is an impressive square tower 85 feet (24 meters) high and is painted with red and white bands.

While the majority of seamarks are placed for use all the year round, some are switched off when the navigation they serve closes because of icy conditions. The lighthouses in the North American Great Lakes, the Baltic Sea, and northern Russian waters all fall into this category. They have to be built to withstand the pressure of ice forming against the structure. One of the most southerly lights in the world flashes out from the Polish Antarctic base at Admiralty Bay on King George Island. Its conspicuous red-and-white-banded steel tower is one of a chain of lights established to help the Antarctic research ships. These lights are operational from November to May during the southern summer.

 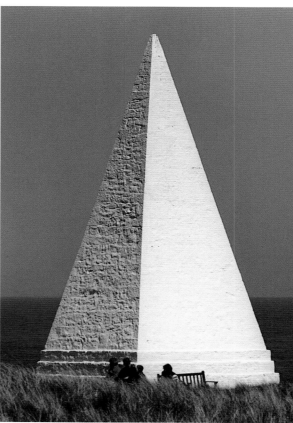 

APPEARANCE IS EVERYTHING

Fog is just as dangerous to the mariner as storms. The flash of the light and the shape and color scheme, no matter how fancy, become useless when they are hidden in the mists, and sound must be used to indicate the lighthouse's position. In early times a cannon or gong was used. The keeper at Boston Lighthouse had to listen for the sound of an incoming vessel's own fog signal. When he heard it he would reply by firing his cannon as a warning to the vessel that it was nearing the lighthouse. It was a hit-and-miss method open to confusion and of little practical use. The early lightships used Chinese gongs. It was a laborious job for the crew yet welcomed by them, because they were paid extra "fog money" during bad visibility. Many ingenious devices were invented to improve the way the sound was generated. The lighthouse at Nidigenen, Sweden, used one of the first fog bells in 1769.

At Bell Rock off the Scottish coast a wind-operated machine operated the bell. The Italians also experimented with wind-machine-driven devices, but the practicality of their use was limited, owing to the fact that quite often fog would roll in on windless days!

Experiments with reed horns were carried out on the foggy East Coast of the U.S. In 1850 C. J. Daboll designed a large reed trumpet measuring 16 feet (5 meters) long with a steel reed tongue in the mouthpiece. The trumpet shape acted like a megaphone to magnify the sound. Daboll's problem, as was the case with other early experimenters, was to get a large enough volume of air passing over the reed. Large bellows were tried but, until the advent of the powered air compressor in the 1890s, the problem remained. The locomotive steam whistle was used at a number of U.S. lighthouses. It was unpopular with the keepers, because they had to get steam up as quickly as possible with the onset of fog. To do this they had to fire up a boiler, and this was both time-consuming and labor-intensive. Sometimes they had to keep up a head of steam for many days.

The use of gas guns was tried in Scotland and Ireland in the 1880s; these used an explosive mixture of acetylene gas and air ignited by a spark from an emery wheel. Operating one was a dangerous and deafening job for the keeper. Smaller automatic versions were used on buoys. In Britain rockets and gun-cotton charges were used. Rockets were mainly used to warn ships away from danger and as distress signals by the keepers. The gun cotton, known as Tonite, was in use at many offshore lighthouses. A 4-ounce (114-gram) Tonite charge was electrically detonated from a jib on the outside of the tower. It took five minutes to reset the charge, which was considered too long, and the idea eventually fell into disfavor.

The New York firm of Brown's developed a siren in 1868 and tested it at Sandy Hook Lighthouse at the southern entrance to the city. It was a successful device using a mechanically driven rotor and a slotted disc to produce a high-pitched sound. The U.S. Lighthouse Service and many other lighthouse authorities adopted the design. It was first used in England at South Foreland Lighthouse and after successful trials and improvements it was used at many other British lighthouses.

The Canadian Lighthouse Service developed the diaphone horn that uses a piston driven by compressed air to make a loud noise, described by some as the noise of a grunting pig! Its use has spread worldwide, because it is a very efficient fog signal. The Typhon fog signal was developed on Sweden and used a vibrating metal diaphragm to produce its sound.

The move to automated lights during the late nineteenth and twentieth centuries led to the development of electrically powered signals that could be operated automatically. The Nautophone, made in Germany, used a magnetic field to excite a vibrating metal diaphragm. In England, Trinity House developed a system that used

BELOW, LEFT TO RIGHT *A fog bell; a 19th-century fog-signal trumpet; a 20th-century electronic fog signal.*

banks of high-frequency loudspeakers. The modern fog signal is an electrically operated diaphragm controlled by an automatic fog-detection device. With all fog signals the aim of the designer is to provide a sound that would not be confused with sounds on board ship and that would travel four to five miles across the sea.

Radio signals were used almost as soon as radio was invented to indicate the position of a lighthouse. A radio transmitter broadcast an identity signal in Morse. This was received on a ship's radio set and by the use of a directional antenna the bearing of the lighthouse could be determined. If bearings of three lighthouses could be obtained, the resulting chart plot would show the ship's position within ½ to 1 mile. This system was first tried using the French lighthouses at Isle Sein and Ushant in 1906 and eventually refined and used throughout the world. (It was discontinued in 1987, when passive racon beacons, or transponders, activated by the approaching ship's own radar equipment, were substituted.)

The Clyde Lighthouse Trust installed a "talking beacon" at Little Cumbrae Lighthouse in Scotland in 1931. This combined a sound signal with a radio signal: the time difference that each type of signal takes to travel a set distance enabled a ship using quite a simple radio receiver to determine its position from the lighthouse.

LISTS OF LIGHTS

All these aids to safe navigation are of little use to the navigator unless recorded, put on charts, and tabulated for reference. Lists of lights have been published almost since there have been lights to list. Alexander George Findlay produced *Lighthouses of the World*, one of the first worldwide lists to be produced. The first edition was published in 1861 and was updated annually for many years. His list for 1874 had over 2,500 entries covering the major and minor lights in 30 countries. Each entry gives the name of the light, its geographical position, details of the light and fog signal, and a brief description of the lighthouse. The U.S. Coastguard and British Hydrographic Office, and the maritime authorities of the major maritime countries, continue to publish annual volumes. To plot the ship's position on the chart using lighthouses, the navigator takes a compass bearing of three adjacent lighthouses. These bearings are transferred to the chart, where the resulting intersection of the bearing lines gives the ship's position.

The advent of the Global Positioning System (GPS) in the latter part of the twentieth century obviated the need for lighthouses by large ships, but they remain as a reassurance that the electronic equipment is working correctly and that the vessel is on a safe course.

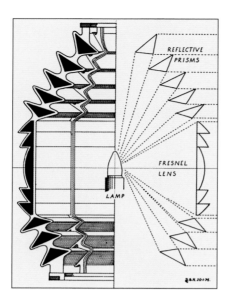

Chapter 3 | LIGHT SOURCES AND LENS SYSTEMS

The type of light shown from the lighthouse tower changed very little in the first 2000 years
of lighthouse development. It was a wood-fired beacon that depended on the vagaries of weather
and the skill of the keeper for its visibility. The lights were good in clear weather
(a well-tended fire could be seen from four or five miles away), but damp conditions
reduced this visibility considerably.

THE EARLY KEEPERS SOON FOUND THAT by gathering the fire into a basket, called a cresset, they obtained better results. ("Cresset," comes ultimately from a Latin word meaning fat, which would have been burned in these containers.) The basket held the fire above the floor, allowing air to be drawn into the embers, making them burn brightly. The cresset used on the Isles of Scilly lighthouse at St. Agnes between 1680 and 1809 remains on display on the adjacent island of Tresco. It is one of the few remaining as a record of this type of basket. While not a particularly efficient way to provide a light, the open fire remained in use in some places until the middle of the nineteenth century. The last in regular use in England was at St. Bees lighthouse on the northeast coast. The cresset was not replaced by oil lamps until 1823. The last in use anywhere in the world is thought to have been the one extinguished at the Norwegian lighthouse at Rundoy in 1858.

Most of the open fires were on flat-topped, open towers with just enough space for the cresset and its immediate fuel supply. On the Baltic coasts the swape light was in more favor. The swape, called by the Danes a *vippefyr*, used

a basket on a long pivoted pole to hold the fire. It was charged with fuel and lit at ground level, then elevated to its working position. Swape lights were used by the Danes well after other countries had established oil-lit towers. A minor swape light was still in use until 1905, operated by Danish Railways on the Island of Gotland. A swape light was placed on Spurn Head at the entrance to the River Humber in England. It was in use for about 80 years until John Smeaton (1724–92), a Yorkshire-born civil engineer, built his much-improved lighthouse. Various ideas were experimented with to improve the quality of the fire. Draft tubes, dampers, and chimneys to control the rate of burning were tried at a number of lighthouses. While the fire was exposed to the elements, most of these flame-enhancing innovations were ineffective, so the idea of enclosing the fire in a glazed chambers was tried. John Smeaton's lighthouse on Spurn Head, which he first lit in 1776, incorporated some of these ideas. Though the controlled-draft coal flame burned much brighter, it was not a complete success because the smoke quickly sooted

RIGHT *Creac'h sur Ouesant (Ushant), France.*

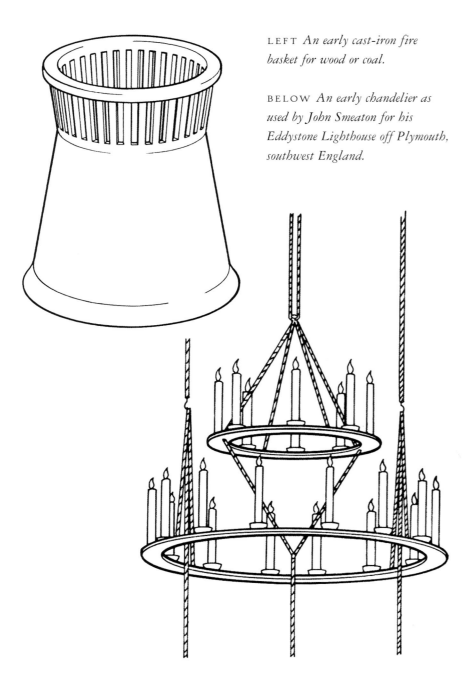

LEFT *An early cast-iron fire basket for wood or coal.*

BELOW *An early chandelier as used by John Smeaton for his Eddystone Lighthouse off Plymouth, southwest England.*

single candle with a reflective surface to gather the backlight. Of the two methods, the reflector light, was the more effective and soon gained favor. With the use of a simple support framework, a number of lamps could be used to give a greater light.

Henry Winstanley, the ship owner (see Chapter 1), favored the chandelier approach at his Eddystone Lighthouse off Plymouth, England. He installed candelabra that held 60 tallow candles that provided a smoky but visible light from the first tower when it was lit on November 14, 1698. Although he was forced to rebuild the tower because of damage after the first winter, his new tower housed the same style of candelabra and remained in use until the tower was destroyed by the Great Storm of 1703.

Candlepower was used in the next tower, built by John Rudyerd in 1706, and was partly responsible for its destruction by fire in 1755. The accumulation of soot and grease had turned the lantern into a firetrap. The 84-year-old keeper, Henry Hall, was startled to find that a fire had started in the lantern. He attempted to unsuccessfully summon his assistants to help him quench the flames. One was drunk and the other took too long to answer the calls for help. The fire gained on Hall in spite of his attempts to put it out. By the time the three men were working together to douse the fire it had started to melt the lead lining of the wooden lantern. While looking up at the blaze, Hall swallowed some of the molten lead. Surprisingly, this did not kill him immediately. He was taken ashore and subsequently died in Plymouth. The lump of lead was removed from his body and is now in the collection of the Royal Society—the independent British body that promotes the natural sciences—in Edinburgh, Scotland. The tower could not be saved, and was left to burn out.

SMEATON STEPS UP

John Smeaton was given the job of building a replacement. His stone tower was a masterpiece of civil engineering. He was determined that it would have an efficient light. First he tried 24 oil lamps, only to find that too much soot was produced. He reverted to using candles, which were in regular use until 1811. Argand oil lamps (named after the eighteenth-century Swiss chemist and inventor Aimé Argand) and reflectors then replaced the 67-candlepower light. This increased the output to 1,125 candlepower, a vast improvement, and for the first time the Eddystone Lighthouse could be seen by the people of Plymouth 14 miles away.

up the lantern glass, reducing the visibility of the flame. Burning coal or wood was very labor-intensive. Even with improved arrangements for fuel and ash handling, it was always backbreaking work to keep the fire burning well. The lighthouse at Spurn Point held over 200 tons of coal. The type of coal used was of a high quality and mined near Newcastle-upon-Tyne, from where it was brought by ship and landed on a nearby beach and carried by oxen to the lighthouse.

Sixteenth-century houses were lit by tallow candles and primitive oil lights, either as single hand lights or large ornate chandeliers. Coal or wood as a fuel on the offshore lighthouses was impracticable, so the early designers built larger versions of the domestic lamps. Their problem was to get enough light from a weak source. This could be achieved in one of two ways: by using either a chandelier, which grouped a large number of candles together, or a

RIGHT *Hutchinson's reflector oil lamp developed at Liverpool, England.*

Plate 10.

BIDSTON LIGHT HOUSE and SIGNALS

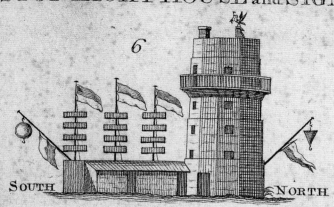

6

SOUTH   NORTH

Vessels coming in

For every
- Ship .... a Board on the South Flag Staff
- Brigg .... D.º .... on the Middle D.º
- Snow Ketch Hoy or large Schooner } .... D.º .... on the North D.º

For more than four Vessels of one kind a Flag on y.º Proper Staff

SIGNALS of DISTRESS

For Vessels in Distress or on shore in y.º Rock Channel or about Hoyle

—— coming in ——

On the Oblique Pole to the Southward of the Light House

For every
- Ship .... a Ball with a Flag half Mast
- Snow .... a Cone broad end up & a Flag half Mast
- Brigg or small Vessel D.º .... small end up & a Flag D.º

—— Going out ——

The same as above but a broad Pendant instead of a Flag

IN FORMBY CHANNEL

—— coming in ——

On the Oblique Pole to the Northward of the Light House

For every
- Ship .... a Ball with a Flag half Mast
- Snow .... a Cone broad end up & a Flag half Mast
- Brigg or small Vessel D.º small end up & a Flag D.º

—— Going out ——

The same as above but a broad Pendant instead of a Flag

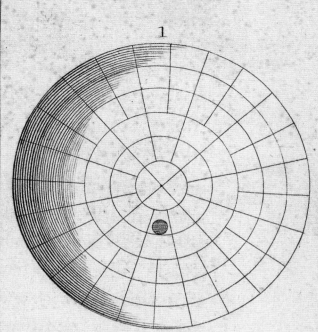

1

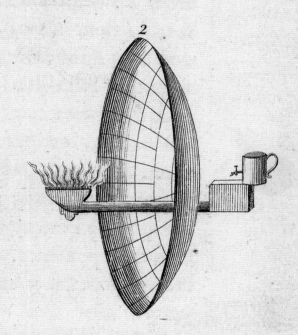

2

3

Focus

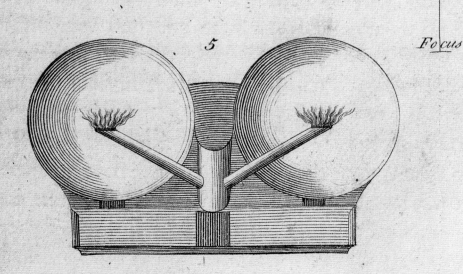

5

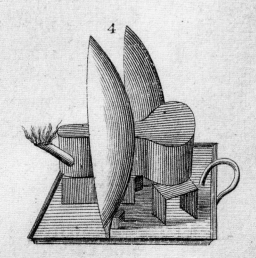

4

A TIME FOR REFLECTION

The earliest record of a reflector light was at the Swedish lighthouse at Landsort between 1669 and 1677; unfortunately for the designer, Johan Braun, the tower burned down and the light was replaced by a coal fire. A century later a Liverpool dockmaster, William Hutchinson, used facets of silvered glass, which he embedded in a parabolic bowl of plaster, at the lighthouse at nearby Bidston. The flame was placed in front of the reflector in such a way that it gathered the rays of light and concentrated them into a beam. The light was produced by a wick floating in a cup in front of the reflector, the oil being fed from a small tank behind the reflector. This was the first attempt at scientific lamp design. His lamps were used for the Smalls Lighthouse off Pembrokeshire, Wales.

Other early equipment makers built on the same idea, improving the optical design by using hollowed copper reflectors that were silvered. Thomas Smith, an oil-lamp maker from Edinburgh, Scotland, perfected the design and methods of manufacture. His machine rolled together sheets of copper and silver. This type of assembly was called the catoptric system (because it involves the concept of reflection), and remained in general use till the nineteenth century.

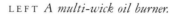

LEFT *A multi-wick oil burner.*

BELOW *The Argand lamp developed in 1781 created an intense, smokeless light equivalent to that of seven candles.*

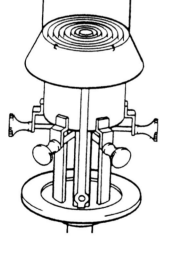

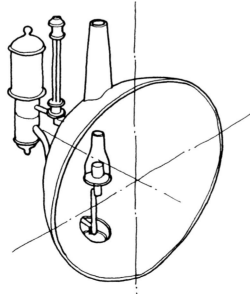

To be effective the reflectors needed to be well made and well maintained. If allowed to dull they were of little use. Single lamps and reflectors were soon replaced by multiple installations to get a greater light output, and the complete assemblies rotated—by clockwork, driven by weights—to give the impression that the light was flashing. Sometimes, on harbor lights, a candle was used instead of an oil cup, but the candle needed constant adjustment if the flame was to stay within the focal plane of the reflector.

Some of the very early lights on the North American shores were wood fires, but these were little more that harbor-marking beacons. The lighthouse built at Little Brewster Island, Boston in 1790 used a "spider" lamp—so called because it looked like a spider. The body was a pan from which four or more flat wicks protruded like a spider's legs. Each wick drew its oil from the pan, burning with an acrid smoky flame. All the early lamps whether spider or cup lamps, were gravity-fed. The early lamp designers had yet to find a method of achieving a regular flow of oil through the wick. Too much oil made a flame too smoky; too little oil gave a poor flame. Choking clouds of smoke caused breathing problems for the keeper as he tried to adjust the lamp, and built up a layer of soot and grease on the reflector and the lantern glazing. John Worthylake, the first keeper on Little Brewster Island, complained regularly about the foul working conditions he experienced when tending the light.

Improving the output of oil lamps taxed many great scientific brains during the eighteenth and nineteenth centuries. Back in the sisteenth century, Leonardo da Vinci had experimented to make the light brighter by fitting a draught tube so that the heat of the flame would draw combustion air over the wick. The French designer Quintquet added a glass chimney to Leonardo's invention around 1775, which, although an improvement, still suffered from the problem of soot. The two ideas used together eventually solved this problem.

The Swiss inventor Aimé Argand made one of the most significant contributions to lighthouse illumination in 1784 with his smokeless lamp. He placed a glass chimney over a cylindrical wick burner, which had its combustion air supplied through its center. The resulting flame was clean and bright. Quickly accepted in the drawing rooms of Europe, it was soon taken up as the major source of light for lighthouses. During the next hundred years his design was universally adopted for all lighthouse lamps. Further developments improved light output and fuel control. Lamps with mechanically operated multi-wick burners using ten concentric wicks, each raised or lowered by rack-and-pinion gearing, were in use at major lighthouses.

The oil used in these first lights was either sperm oil, extracted from the head of the sperm whale, or colza oil made from the wild cabbage plant. Both were difficult to obtain in large quantities, and were therefore expensive. Many other types of oil were experimented with, and some quite strange substances were tried occasionally with surprising results. For instance, oils were extracted from a variety of vegetables and fruits, olives, seed pods, and fish. Sometimes, for local expediency, these oils were adopted in spite of high cost. In the 1840s, three lighthouses in South Africa's Cape Province used oil obtained from the gland above the tail of the Cape sheep. Though it was expensive to obtain because only a small amount could be extracted at a time, and needed twice the quantity of colza oil because it was more volatile, that volatility gave it a brilliant flame. The lighthouse keeper at Cape Hatteras, North Carolina, was ordered in 1803 to experiment with porpoise oil. It was not adopted for regular use, because the flame was considered too small and supplies were limited.

Sperm oil was adopted for general use in most countries, with colza oil in favor where its cabbage-plant derivative was grown, particularly in France. The United States

ABOVE *A whale oil lighthouse lamp from 1763.*

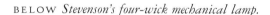

BELOW *Stevenson's four-wick mechanical lamp.*

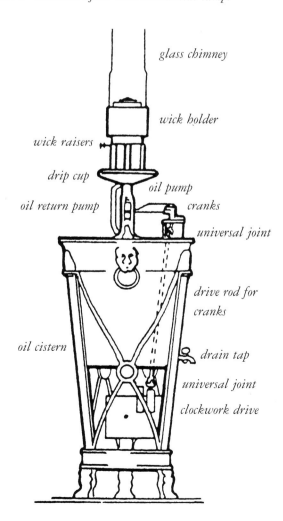

glass chimney

wick holder

wick raisers

drip cup

oil pump

oil return pump

cranks

universal joint

drive rod for cranks

oil cistern

drain tap

universal joint

clockwork drive

Lighthouse Board tried, without success, to get American farmers to grow the crop so that they would be less dependent on the sperm-oil market. Some oils tended to become too viscous when cold. Lard oil was readily available but not used for many years because it solidified quickly in the winter. Occasionally, earth oil was used when it could be obtained; natural deposits were found in Burma and Venezuela, where it bubbled to the surface. Charles Stevenson, the Scottish lighthouse engineer, reported on a visit he made in 1874 to a factory in West Lothian, Scotland, making lamp oil by processing shale-oil rocks. The resulting oil was similar to modern kerosene.

The discovery of earth oil in Pennsylvania in August 1859 by Edwin Drake had revolutionized domestic lighting long before its use in industry and transport was considered. The refinement of crude oil into cheap kerosene ensured that oil lamps and cooking stoves, hitherto luxuries, quickly became mass consumer items. This cheap lamp oil was shipped all over the world from the U.S.A., first in tins and as demand grew by tankers. Its availability led to an explosive growth in the development of the oil lamp. While the well-tried Argand lamp still held sway in lighthouse illumination, inventors and lamp makers were incorporating new and novel ideas to make better, more reliable, and cheaper lamps available. In

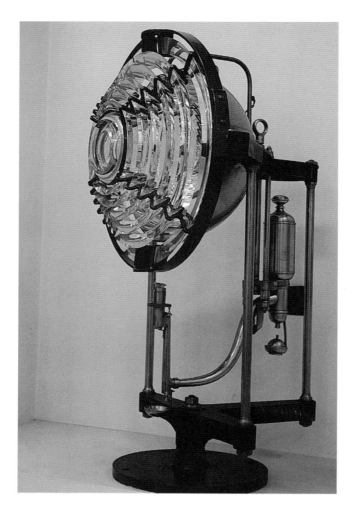

Austria a young chemist, Carl Auer von Welsbach, perfected a mantle in about 1885 that, when fixed over a naked flame, caused incandescence, and increased the light output by three times. Initially, the mantle was made for gaslights but was soon adopted for use with oil lamps.

Two American lamp makers almost dominated the lighting market. Arthur Kitson started manufacturing incandescent oil lamps to his own design in Philadelphia in 1896. He took the idea of the Welsbach mantle, allied it to the concept behind Robert Wilhelm Bunsen's controlled gas-air burner so familiar in laboratories, and added his own patent way of vaporizing oil. The resulting lamp gave a light that was clean bright and very economic in use. Its use spread quickly in home and industry; not surprisingly, lighthouse engineers soon adopted it.

Arthur Kitson chose to use pressure rather than capillary action to transfer the fuel from the storage tank to the burner. By the addition of a small hand pump to the tank, the fuel could be fed to the atomizing chamber without the need for a wick. This method permitted precise control and created a much more powerful flame. The downside was the roar of the lamp when in operation. Though the noise was unacceptable in domestic situations, the output was six times that of a wick burner, making it ideal for lighthouse application.

ABOVE LEFT *A Stevenson-designed dioptric holophote lens dating from 1849.*

ABOVE *A compound oil burner.*

RIGHT *Elbow Reef Lighthouse, Bahamas — the last in the world to use a Kitson-type, pressurized-vapor, kerosene burner.*

FAR RIGHT, FROM TOP TO BOTTOM *The winding gear, lens, and pressure tanks at Elbow Reef.*

Lighthouse authorities, including Trinity House in the U.K., very quickly adopted Kitson's paraffin vapor burner (PVB). They were later, in 1921, to benefit from their early experience when their chief engineer, David Hood, perfected the oil burner. Hood's own PVB lamp was to remain the mainstay of their lights until it was superseded by the electric-filament bulb.

The last Kitson PVB lamp was extinguished as recently as 1977, when Trinity House electrified their lighthouse on St. Mary's Island in Northumberland. The lamp had been in use every night, except for short times during the two World Wars, since first lit in 1898. A paraffin vapor burner is still in nightly use at Elbow Reef Lighthouse in the Bahamas.

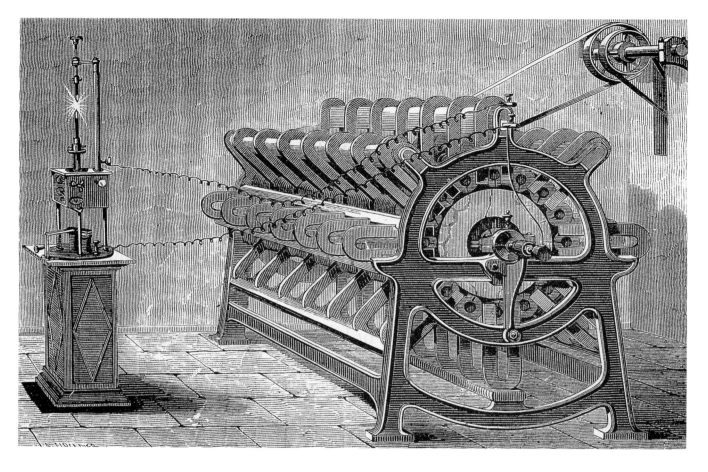

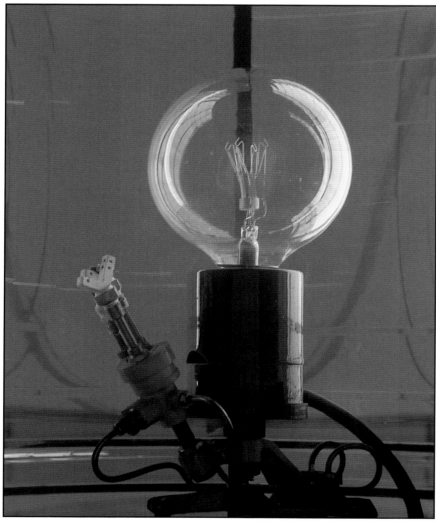

Mention must be made of the world-famous Aladdin Company. The Aladdin engineers produced a lamp in 1709 that was quiet and simple in operation. The paraffin was drawn up the flat wick by capillary action into a chamber where, heat allowed it to vaporize. The gas produced burned on the outside of the mantle. Many Aladdin lamps were used in lighthouses and on board lightships, as well as for domestic lighting and as standby lights in case of the failure of the main light.

THE AGE OF GAS

Parallel with the improvement in oil lights was the use of gas. Gas was a substitute for the early oils, but, with the exception of the widespread use of acetylene, gas lost favor with lighthouse engineers when paraffin became readily available. The first use of gas from coal was for lighting. The streets of London were lit in 1807, Baltimore in 1816, and New York in 1837. It was in general home use by the mid-1860s, with most towns having their own gas works.

Salvatore lighthouse at Trieste, Italy, used a gas light in 1818. The open gas jets were mounted on a tiered chandelier within a glazed lantern. Although this was ventilated, the heat produced must have been a problem to the keepers and the structure. In 1821, the Scottish-born civil engineer John Rennie (1761–1821) built a pier and a lighthouse at Holyhead in North Wales; both were lit by gas. The enterprise was fraught with danger, and resulted in many accidents. On one occasion the attendant approached the "empty" gasholder while holding a candle and was killed by the resulting explosion. In 1866, John Wigham, the Irish lighthouse engineer, built a small gasworks to light Howth Baily at the entrance to Dublin Bay.

In the United States, rural people in the main used oil lighting and wood for heating and cooking until the end of the 19th century. This was reflected in the somewhat conservative attitude of the lighthouse authorities to the use of gas. They did not eagerly welcome change. However

TOP LEFT *An early experiment in lighthouse electricity. Professor Holmes' Electrical Generator provided power to the carbon arc lamp.*

FAR LEFT *The novel use of both gas and electricity—the large bulb is the main electrically powered light source. When the lamp or the electrical supply failed, a detector automatically moved the gas lamp into the correct place and ignited it to maintain the light. The gas was supplied from storage cylinders.*

LEFT *An example of Dalens automatic mantle changer.*

ABOVE *A keeper undertaking the laborious, sometimes hourly, task of winding the weights.*

Stephen Pleasonton, the U.S. Treasury official responsible for lighthouses, did authorize some experimental installations at three lighthouses in Delaware Bay in the North Atlantic. They were not successful, as a result not of poor equipment but the attitude of the keepers. They allowed the gas-making retorts to burn out before asking for replacements. When they were supplied with a backup plant, the keepers still allowed the equipment to fail so that they could revert to the oil lamps. Pleasonton concluded that their attitude was deliberate, because they disliked the labor involved in operating the gas-making plant. He also tested natural gas that had been found near to Portland on the shores of Lake Erie. The Barcelona Lighthouse near Portland was lit in 1829 but was never successful, because the two-mile pipeline from the source of the gas collected water and had to be repeatedly lifted and drained. The light was discontinued in 1859, when it was decided that it was of no further use.

Gas was also made from a number of other substances. The Finnish lighthouse at Porkkala, for instance, used a gas made by heating pinewood. Germany used compressed-oil gas, water gas (made by passing steam over red-hot coke and producing a mixture of hydrogen and carbon monoxide), and an important development, Blau gas. This was the first gas to be liquefied and transported in high-pressure cylinders. It was used to light buoys and was also used in Poland at Pillau, where the lighthouse was the first one to operate without permanent keepers on duty.

In Canada, Thomas Willson, an inventor, found a way in 1892 to manufacture acetylene gas using calcium carbide. He employed a simple water generator to produce a low-pressure and easily controlled gas. The gas was first used in industrial processes such as welding. Gas was generated and distributed within the workshop by low-pressure pipes. In 1896, two French chemists, George Claude and Albert Hess, found that, by dissolving the gas in acetone, they could carry it in steel cylinders.

The ease with which acetylene could be made and transported revolutionized many processes in the early part of the twentieth century. Portable gas-powered equipment was quickly developed. Its use in navigation attracted simultaneous work in Sweden and Canada. Willson had found a

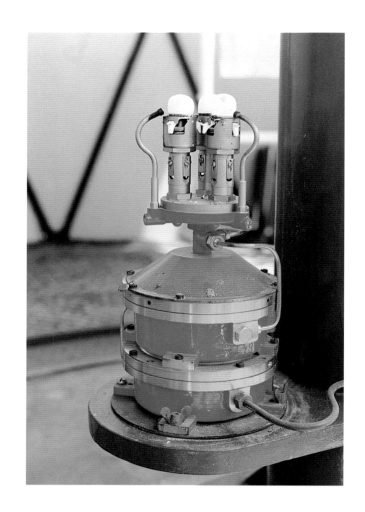

RIGHT *A modern gas mantle lamp like that in use at Chicken Rock Lighthouse, Isle of Man.*

BELOW *Lighthouse keeper Bill Bemister checking the modern acrylic lens light unit at Boat Bluff Lighthouse, British Columbia, Canada.*

way to generate the gas within the body of a buoy, and, by 1911, there were more than 250 acetylene buoys operating in Canadian waters.

The Swedish lighthouse engineer, John Höjer, had been tasked with providing navigation lights for the indented coastline. Because of the number of lights needed, he was attracted to the idea that as many as possible should work without the need for keepers, by having the fuel burn continuously (a group of lights would have an attendant, who would visit on a regular basis). This would cut down costs, and enable him to place lights in remote places. By using acetylene gas in cylinders, he resolved the problem of his fuel supply, because enough fuel could be transported and stored at the lighthouse sites for use over a long period.

Trials began, but not without problems. The early cylinders were liable to explode. The fuel gave a good clean light, but was proving expensive, because it was burned continuously. It was also a fixed light, unlike those in major manned lighthouses, where manually wound clockwork systems were used to operate shutters or cause the light assembly to rotate to give the impression of a flashing light. In 1904, Höjer talked his problems over with a fellow Swede, Gustaf Dalen, who had recently founded the Gasaccumulator Company (later to be the well-known AGA Company).

THE FIRST FULLY AUTOMATIC LIGHTHOUSE

Dalen's prolific mind and technical skill gave the world its first fully automatic lighthouse in 1910 on Sweden's southeast coast. But first he had to solve the three main problems of unwanted explosions, using an expensive fuel economically, and making the light flash. He improved the way in which the dissolved gas mixture was held in the storage cylinder by adding a ceramic "sponge," which made it explosion-proof. He designed a flashing apparatus that not only saved fuel but also enabled the light to be given an individual character. This he did using a small economic pilot light to ignite bursts of gas; thus he was able to arrange any combination of light and dark periods. His next idea was to be able to make the gas flow by night and stop by day. The resulting "sun valve" was at first greeted with disbelief and some derision. A black rod inserted into a glass casing with two reflective bars expanded when heated, causing a valve to close and the gas supply to be cut off (this was achieved by the differential expansion of the black rod and the reflective bars); conversely at night it cooled and allowed the gas to flow. The combination of these two techniques meant that the light now used less that 10 percent of its fuel store, so that a cylinder that had lasted less that one month now held enough for a whole year's supply.

ABOVE *The Dalen automatic gas mantle changer was last in use at Caldy Island Lighthouse, Wales. This was changed to electric light in 1998.*

Dalen's work was not limited to lighthouse equipment. In homes over the world his AGA cookers and heating stoves are known and loved. With his other commitments he still found time to explore ways to improve his lights, which were now in general use with lighthouse authorities for lighthouses and buoys. He wanted to increase the light output from his existing equipment to enable small units to have increased luminosity. He experimented with a mantle that handled an explosive gas/air mixture but gave a bright, concentrated light source. To remove the danger, he evolved an explosion-proof mixer valve. He also found a way of using the gas pressure to revolve the lens around the mantle. Because of the limited life and possible failure of the mantle, he added an ingenious mechanism allowed a worn or damaged mantle to be automatically replaced by a good one. The AGA light system proved to have complete reliability. Thousands of installations are left untended for up to twelve months. The Karlskrona Lighthouse on Sweden's southeast coast was the first fully automatic major lighthouse. The AGA Company supplied lighting for many major installations. The company lit both the Suez and Panama Canals, the latter its largest single contract.

Lighthouse illumination was no longer a hit-and-miss affair. Engineers fitting out new lighthouses could choose from pressurized-vapor burners using paraffin, AGA automatic gaslights using acetylene, and, increasingly, electricity as reliable light sources. Electricity was experimented with by many nineteenth-century scientists and engineers, but for many years it was no more that a laboratory toy. The English chemist Sir Humphry Davy (1778–1829) made an electric arc light as early as 1805 but it was another 50 years before the generation of electricity was advanced enough to be considered for lighthouse use.

FARADAY'S CARBON ARCS

Professor Michael Faraday (1791–1867), the British physicist and chemist, was the scientific adviser to Trinity House during the 1860s. He suggested that trials using a carbon arc lamp should be instituted, since its light source should be ideal for lighthouses. Carbon arc lamps were fitted at Dungeness and Souter Lighthouses—in Kent in the south and the northeast coast of England respectively—but the short duration of the flash proved unacceptable and the lights reverted to oil lamps in the 1870s.

Although in 1878 both Thomas Edison in the United States and Joseph Swan in Britain developed the light bulb

BELOW *The east elevation of Souter Point Lighthouse in 1873.*

RIGHT *An 1874 chart illustrating the sectors and ranges of the experimental electric light at Souter Point Lighthouse in 1873.*

we are familiar with, it was not until the 1920s that electric lamps were used in lighthouses. The early filament bulbs were not reliable, because they suffered from poor vacuum and filament burn, causing the light to deteriorate during its relatively short life. The advent of tungsten filaments and improved manufacturing methods eventually enabled the production of reliable high-output bulbs. The changeover from PV burners to electric bulbs took many years, but was the start of a general move towards the total automation of aids to navigation. Many land lighthouse now take their electricity from national power grids, while those offshore have either constantly running generators that need little maintenance or, increasingly, use solar and/or wind power to charge batteries for lamps and operate services.

Another form of energy for the power source has, of course, been nuclear. An experimental nuclear generator was installed in 1964 at the Baltimore Lighthouse, but was removed after two years of unsuccessful operation. One of the problems was unreliability, and another was a suspicion of nuclear energy. In Ireland the lighthouse at Rathlin O'Birne was for many years powered by a small thermonuclear generator, which charged low-voltage batteries. This interesting installation used a low-voltage lamp array of 36 tungsten-halogen bulbs. Each was fitted in a reflector with automatic changeover in case of failure. The lamp array was rotated using a low-consumption, gearless, rotating motor. The AGA Company designed the complete system after they became general lighthouse engineers. Small metal halogen bulbs have almost replaced the large filament light bulbs, because they can be run at low voltages from batteries. While the modern lighthouse has retained the lantern tower and original lens system, the light source and all the associated control equipment are low-voltage. The development of the fully electrified automatic lighthouse began in the 1930s in the United States, but the keepers remained part of the lighthouse scene in many countries until 1999. Most operators have elected to have each lighthouse run as an independent unit, visited on a regular basis by a technician to carry

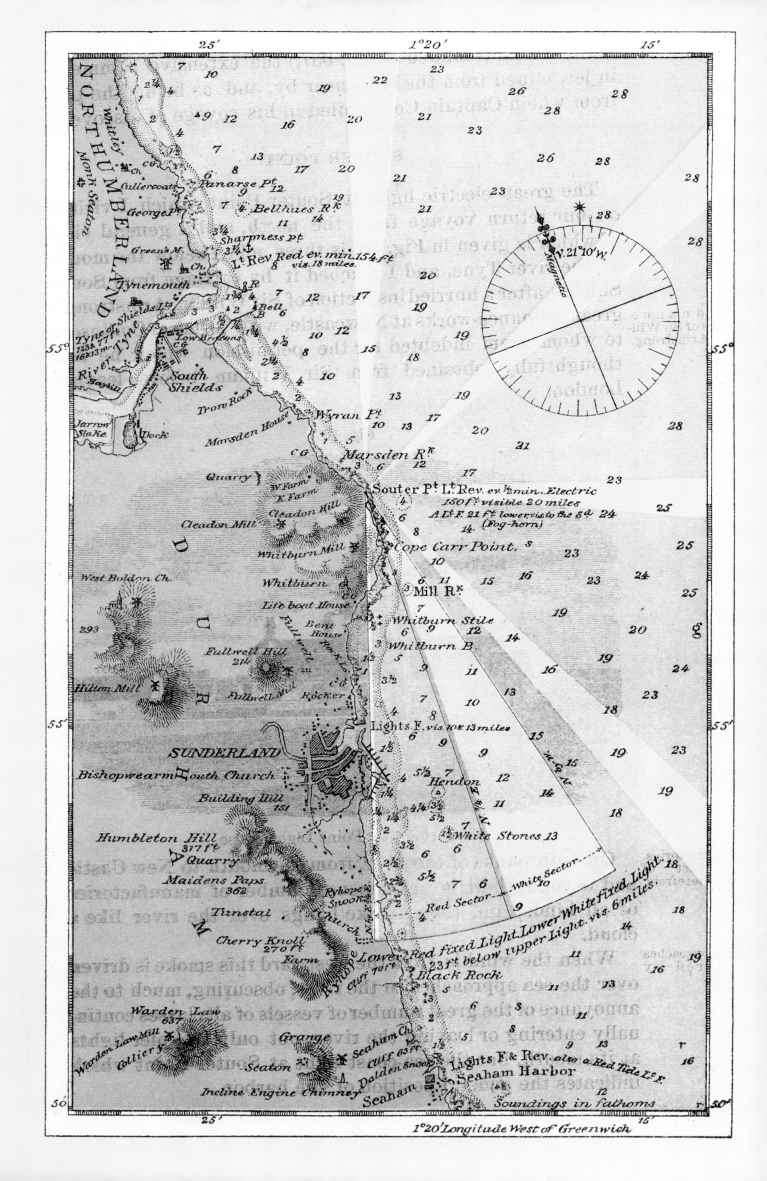

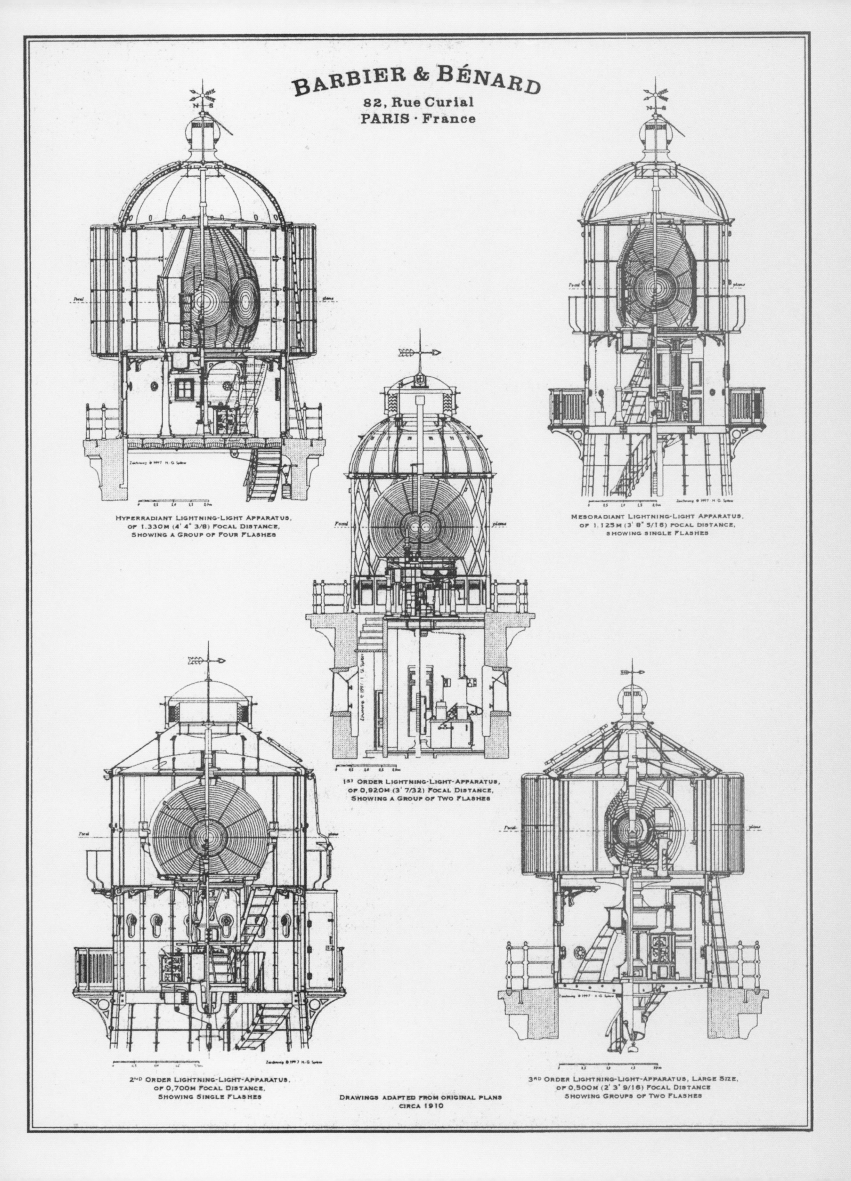

BARBIER & BÉNARD
82, Rue Curial
PARIS · France

HYPERRADIANT LIGHTNING-LIGHT APPARATUS,
OF 1.330M (4' 4" 3/8) FOCAL DISTANCE,
SHOWING A GROUP OF FOUR FLASHES

MESORADIANT LIGHTNING-LIGHT APPARATUS,
OF 1.125M (3' 8" 5/16) FOCAL DISTANCE,
SHOWING SINGLE FLASHES

1ST ORDER LIGHTNING-LIGHT-APPARATUS,
OF 0.920M (3' 7/32) FOCAL DISTANCE,
SHOWING A GROUP OF TWO FLASHES

2ND ORDER LIGHTNING-LIGHT-APPARATUS,
OF 0.700M FOCAL DISTANCE,
SHOWING SINGLE FLASHES

DRAWINGS ADAPTED FROM ORIGINAL PLANS
CIRCA 1910

3RD ORDER LIGHTNING-LIGHT-APPARATUS, LARGE SIZE,
OF 0.500M (2' 3" 9/16) FOCAL DISTANCE
SHOWING GROUPS OF TWO FLASHES

out maintenance or when passing ships report that the light has gone out. Others have elected for centralized control, using either radio telemetry or telephone lines to link a remote interface to a central control.

Scotland's Northern Lighthouse Board is an example of the latter: most of its 200 automatic lighthouses are monitored from Edinburgh. The duty controller has a computer screen that indicates that the light and its fog signal (if fitted) are operating correctly; it also advises on the integrity of the station and its buildings in case of fire or intruder. The controller is able to send signals back to the lighthouse to override local actions or correct malfunctions. The stations have attendants from the local community who visit on a regular basis to carry out cleaning and minor maintenance tasks.

The fuel and the way it was converted into a light source are only part of the quest to light the mariner's way. Projecting the light so that it was visible was also subject of much trial and error. The early lights were soon enclosed in lantern houses, their design never drastically changing. There were improvements in glazing and ventilation, but the shape and purpose of the lantern house from 1600 onward remains recognizable even in the twenty-first century. Until the advent of wrought iron, the lanterns, even those with coal fires, were timber-built, although the better ones were lead-lined for safety.

The greatest change came in the nineteenth century, with the magnificent cast- and wrought-iron work of the birdcage, or diamond-shaped glazing bars, known as astragals, supporting large areas of glass. To enable the keepers to clean the outside, galleries and handholds became part of the design, which was often topped with an ornate weathervane.

STRIVING FOR A BRIGHTER LIGHT

While much of the emphasis on the development of lighthouse illumination naturally concerned the fuel and the way that it was burned, attention was given finding methods of improving the projection of the light. Reflectors were widely used, but later inventors strove to magnify the lights. The magnifying effect of the "bull's eye" formed during the manufacture of the early sheet glass was well known. Thomas Rogers in Britain and Captain Winslow Lewis in the United States both attempted to increase the light with the addition of a bull's-eye lens in front of the

LEFT An engraving by Hans-Guenter Spitzer from the original Barbier and Bénard, Paris, catalog. Their range of lighthouse optics were extensively used by the United States Lighthouse Board during the ninteenth century.

ABOVE *1200 watt MBI lamp bulb.*

light—Thomas in the late 1780s and Lewis from around 1810. The thickness of the glass and its impurities lessened the light considerably so the idea was abandoned. The magnifying lens tried by Winslow Lewis was said to be made of thick green glass.

Multiple Argand lamp-and-reflector assemblies were the mainstay of lighthouse illumination until the French physicist Augustin Fresnel (1788–1827) invented his circular lens system, which gave a concentrated beam from a single light source. Fresnel was a member of the French Lighthouse Commission, and was concerned about the limitations and imperfections in the existing catoptric (or reflection) system. The size of lights was limited by the weight of mirrors, which also absorbed too much of the lamp's output. He decided that a lens was required that would intensify and concentrate the light into a beam so that the heavy reflector could be dispensed with. Although he was not the first to consider the problem, he was the first to turn theory into practice.

Buffon and De Condercet in France and Sir David Brewster (1761–1868) in Britain (he was the inventor of the kaleidoscope and a founder member of the British

ABOVE *The keeper at Cape Finisterre, Spain, fitting a new lamp bulb.*

BELOW *The lantern house of Heceta Head Lighthouse with its first-order Fresnel lens that was fitted in 1894, converted to automatic in 1963, and is still in use.*

RIGHT *St Simon's Island Light, Georgia.*

Association for the Advancement of Science in 1831) had all theorized about the use of polished prism-shaped lens elements. Fresnel's system was quite simple: he took a bull's-eye lens and fitted concentric glass rings round it to make a thin lightweight construction. This allowed 90 percent of the light to pass through, compared with 50 percent using the catoptric system.

Because the new design, called a dioptric system, was light in weight, it was possible for Fresnel to assemble lens panels into sets and place them around a single central light source. At the same time, a better light with multiple beams was produced, which, when rotated, appeared as flashes.

The first lighthouse to benefit from the new design was Cordouan in western France in 1823. Fresnel did not live to see the growth of his lenses or the further work to improve them by the builder of Skerryvore Lighthouse, Alan Stevenson, and James Timmins Chance, whose father founded the Birmingham glassmaking company of that name. They perfected the catadioptric systems, in which mirrored prisms gathered all the vestiges of wasted light and returned it into the light path to intensify the main beam. Augustin Fresnel's brother, Leonor, continued his work when he joined Cookson's of Newcastle-upon-Tyne. They supplied Fresnel lens units for 15 British lighthouses before they closed down in 1845. Their demise left Chance Bros. of Birmingham, England, and Letourneau & Lepaute of Paris, France, to dominate lighthouse optical

manufacturing, which they continued to do for many years. The lighthouse equipment from these two companies is still in worldwide use, much of it the original equipment, but enhanced with modern technology.

The adoption of the Fresnel lens in the United States was much slower than elsewhere, for many reasons. Winslow Lewis had introduced his version of the Argand lamp and reflector to the Lighthouse Board in 1810. He was given the contract to fit one at the Boston Lighthouse. His claim that his system produced a brighter light using half the amount of oil was acknowledged to be correct by the board, who proceeded to give him most of their lighthouse-illumination business. This led to allegations of corrupt practice. He had a virtual monopoly for 25 years in spite of claims of poor quality and price fixing.

THE BOARD PRESSURES CONGRESS

Because there were no American makers of optical glass, the U.S. Treasury was forced to obtain Fresnel lenses from Europe. Although the Treasury had resisted, evidence was laid before Congress that ships' masters had logged that the lights exhibited by European lighthouses were far superior to those shown by their own lighthouses. As a result, Commodore Matthew Perry was sent to verify the claims and find out more about the European systems. He returned home with two Fresnel lenses, which were installed in the twin towers of Navesink Lighthouse, New Jersey, in 1840. Though they proved to be better, lethargy and maladministration by the department within the Treasury concerned with lighthouses prevailed. By 1851 Congress was totally dissatisfied with they way its lighthouses were being administered. To resolve the situation, a board of investigation was set up to review the work of the administrators and keepers, and to visit and inspect lighthouses. It found many problems, including the fact that most lighthouses, except for the few with Fresnel lenses, were worse than useless. One comment was, "The lights are so bad that the lights south of Navesink were virtually useless to the mariner."

After receiving the board's report, Congress reorganized the administration of lighthouses under a new United States Lighthouse Board, and, importantly, mandated that Fresnel lenses be fitted at all the lighthouses. The new board was made up of people who had served on the investigation. They quickly set to work to remedy the situation by ordering lenses from France. Although this was expensive and frustrating, owing to high cost of shipping and delays caused by breakage during transit, all the lights were converted by the start of the Civil War. Because of war damage to some of the lights, the board returned to Europe for new ones, because no American manufacturer could supply their requirements. This was unfortunate because, as systems for repair were shipped overseas, new equipment was delayed or arrived damaged, causing long and frustrating delays. The situation was only partly resolved when the Macbeth-Evans Company started making small Fresnel lens units for lightships in 1910.

BELOW *First-order Fresnel lens system removed from Anvil Point Lighthouse, Dorset, England. Now on display in London's Science Museum.*

TOP LEFT *Third-order Fresnel lens at Split Rock Lighthouse, Minnesota.*

LEFT *Trinity House Light Vessels use a variety of lamp configurations. The reflector system shown here was used on LV15, which has retained this unique light source despite being out of service, and is now used as a Christian Youth Training Center on the Essex marshes, north of London.*

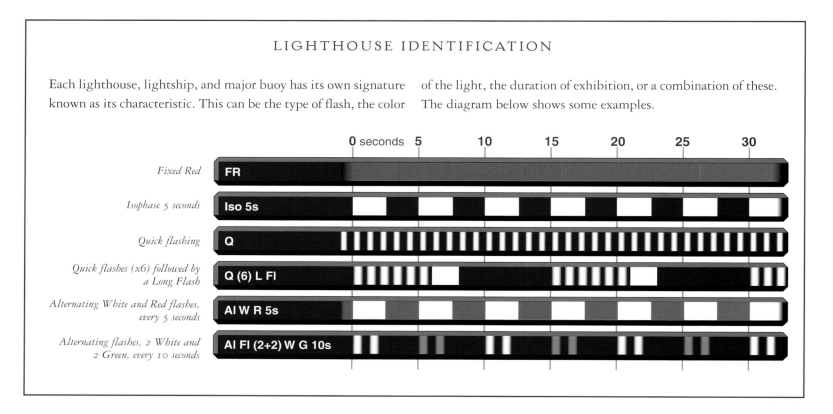

LIGHTHOUSE IDENTIFICATION

Each lighthouse, lightship, and major buoy has its own signature known as its characteristic. This can be the type of flash, the color of the light, the duration of exhibition, or a combination of these. The diagram below shows some examples.

George Macbeth (1845–1916) began glass making in Indiana and later in Pittsburgh, Pennsylvania. In 1872 he was manufacturing glass chimneys for oil lamps, and by 1880 he was one of the world's largest producers of lamp chimneys. In 1899, Macbeth Glass merged with a competitor, Thomas Evans Glass, to become Macbeth-Evans, and the firm became the largest producer of glass chimneys, as well as many other glass products.

Although they were the largest company in the world making glass chimneys for oil lamps, their optical glass output was very small, largely due to uncompetitive prices caused by high labor costs in the United States, compared with those in Europe.

Fresnel lenses were made in standard sizes, which are referred to as "orders." The focal distance is used as the yardstick measurement. The first order measured just over 36 inches (920 millimeters), while the smallest harbor light, a sixth-order light, was less than 6 inches (150 millimeters). When the very powerful oil lamps with as many as seven rings of wicks were designed, even larger focal lengths were needed to accommodate them, so lenses called hyper-radial (just over 52 inches, or 1,330 millimeters) and meso-radial (about 44 inches, or 1,120 millimeters) were developed. Other variations were engineered by the optical designers. By mounting two systems one on top of the other, a biform optic could be assembled. This form was used at the Eddystone Lighthouse off Plymouth, England, when the fifth tower was equipped with a 12-sided, first-order biform lens. It was arranged to rotate once every three minutes, giving the impression of two flashes every thirty seconds.

The unit, weighing about six tons, was mounted on rollers and powered by falling weights that were rewound by the keeper at frequent intervals.

As with any moving mechanism, friction was always a problem with large heavy units. It slowed things down. The engineers at Chance Bros. developed a method of using mercury as a bearing for these heavy optical structures. The optic was floated in a bath of mercury, reducing friction so much that the five-ton optics could be rotated by finger pressure alone during cleaning. Operationally, this meant smaller driving weights for the clockwork system, less rewinding, and faster lens rotation. The Chance engineers used this attribute to build optic systems with groups of quick-flashing beams. Until electronic light switching came along, this was the ultimate in controlling flashing. The ability to change from a fixed light to a recognizable flashing characteristic had been a problem for three hundred years of lighthouse engineering. Now it was much easier.

However, the cresset and candle towers were difficult to identify individually, because each light appeared the same from the sea. The approaches to New York in the early 1800s illustrate the problem. Navesink Lighthouse, erected in 1828, had lights on towers placed about 395 feet (120 meters) apart. Its neighbor at Sandy Hook, already in existence since 1782, showed its single light from a similar tower. Later, two more lights were added: one on the original tower and a beacon a quarter of a mile away. The light vessel anchored six miles to the north of the spit displayed two red lights. The approaching navigator was supposed to see two lights side by side to indicate the position of the Navesink light, a triangular array for Sandy Hook, and two red lights arranged vertically for the light vessel. In poor weather conditions, it was very confusing.

Lack of knowledge by the builder, site considerations, or economics caused many towers to be built too close together. The Gurnet lights at the entrance to Plymouth Bay, Massachusetts, were set only 33 feet (10 meters) apart. A lighthouse inspector noted that this showed as one light when viewed from seaward. Triple lights were used at the Casquets lightship in the Channel Islands off the French coast to differentiate them from the twin Lizard lights off Cornwall, England. They too were ineffective. There are many other examples.

FLASH OF INSPIRATION

The first light to use flashing was a rotating catoptric system fitted at Carlsten Lighthouse in Sweden by Jonas Norberg in 1781. His method was to arrange the reflectors on a stand so that a clockwork motor could rotate them. This allowed the light to be followed by darkness as the reflector turned away from view. This system was successfully used at the lighthouses in Dieppe, northern France, and Liverpool in the northwest of England. Cordouan Lighthouse in western France had a similar system, using 24 Argand lamps and reflectors fitted in 1790. This partly resolved the problem of giving lights a characteristic flash, but the need was to control the lights, so that there were enough variations to ensure that a coastline would have each light as distinctive by night as it was by day. Around 1865, Carl Gustaf von Otter tried clockwork-driven Venetian blinds that he could arrange to open and close at predetermined intervals. There were many variations on the clockwork theme. Some worked, but many were mechanical contrivances beloved only by the inventor. As we have already noted, the Fresnel lens system helped to perfect the use of the required variation in light characteristics. It is interesting to see that some of the early ideas are still used in modern lamp arrays.

Today's optical assemblies rely on the developments of the early pioneers. The modern polycarbonate-molded optic in use in many North American lighthouses still has the lens configuration first thought of by Fresnel. Many lighthouses have their original lens systems fitted with modern, automated, low-power, high-intensity lamps.

When we think of today's modern lighthouse technology, we mustn't forget that the later innovators were, as Isaac Newton might have said, standing on the shoulders of giants. What we see today would not have been possible without the invention and determination of those pioneers.

RIGHT *The loom of Bodie Island light.*

Chapter 4 | DESIGNERS AND BUILDERS

Many of the early lighthouses, when Britain and France were world leaders in lighthouse design, were built by men with more vision than apparent skills. A musical-instrument maker, Henry Whiteside, probably from the Liverpool area of England, was one of the more enigmatic characters. His introduction to lighthouse building happened in the 1770s because John Phillips, the Liverpool dockmaster, gave him the task of making a model of a proposed lighthouse at the Skerries in the approaches to the port. Nothing is known about the model, and the lighthouse to the Phillips design was never built. In 1773, Phillips again approached Whiteside with a proposal that the instrument maker design and build a lighthouse for the Smalls Reef. This reef, 20 miles off the Welsh coast, was a constant danger to ships making for Liverpool further north, and needed a light to warn shipping of its presence. Whiteside designed an ingenious timber tower, made a model of it, and, when work started on the reef in 1774, he supervised the building work and stayed on the lighthouse to observe that it worked as he wished. This, the first timber pile lighthouse, lasted 87 years until it was demolished to make way for a new conventional stone tower, which remains in use today.

LIGHTHOUSE ENGINEERS WERE typically self-taught constructors of the practical school, who also studied natural philosophies, math, and sciences and took a lively interest in the ways of nature. They were educated men who chose to take on nature in order to put lighthouses on foundations that were often underwater and at inaccessible locations. They endured great hardship, even for the times that they lived in. Their shared attribute seemed to be that they were all determined to beat seemingly impossible odds. They did this with courage, patience, and endurance, using their self-acquired skills and a natural management ability of which modern multinational companies would be proud.

The Stevenson dynasty of lighthouse builders, based in Scotland, contributed five generations to lighthouse service. Their contribution started with the building of five coastal lighthouses on the Scottish coast, beginning in 1787 and ending with the building of Esha Ness Lighthouse in 1929, though some minor lights were built right up to the day the last family member retired in 1938. Their work touched every continent as they built

RIGHT *Lighthouses built on offshore rocks have to withstand the onslaught of the weather. The power of the waves hitting this French lighthouse at La Jument off the Brittany coast causes even this massive tower to vibrate.*

ABOVE *When Robert Stevenson built the Bell Rock Lighthouse off the Scottish coast, he needed to erect a refuge and living quarters for the builders even before he started work on the lighthouse.*

lighthouses and carried out consultancy on a wide range of engineering projects. Their prolific writing and lecturing about lighthouses and civil engineering was required study for every lighthouse engineer. Each generation was at the leading edge of the technology of the day. They read and traveled widely to keep abreast of the work of others, but were all devoted family men who also used their skills away from civil engineering for the benefit of church and fellow human beings.

To familiarize ourselves with the Stevenson dynasty, we must go back to a small coastal village near Dundee and the birth there in 1752, of Thomas Smith, the man generally accepted as its founder. This bright, intelligent boy with a flair for practical work was apprenticed at the age of 12 to a Dundee metalworker. He learned his trade and then decided to seek his fortune in Edinburgh. He arrived in the capital in 1770 to work for the city's leading oil-lamp maker. By 1781 he had started a business on his own account, making oil lamps and domestic brasswork.

The business thrived and grew, soon needing larger premises. Despite being so busy, Smith also found time to marry twice—losing both wives and four children—before he eventually met and married his third wife, Jane Stevenson, on November 14, 1792. This union was to produce the famed Stevenson dynasty.

Smith did not let his family life detract from his business. Indeed, he was now Scotland's principal lighting manufacturer. In 1787 he had won the street-lighting contract from Edinburgh Town Council, and followed it with contracts for many other cities and towns throughout Scotland. His price of 6 pence per street lamp was very competitive, but his company's manufacturing skills, allied to his commercial expertise, made him good profits. He could afford to experiment with new ideas for lighting, and indulge his interest in using oil lights for harbor and coastal lights. He developed lamps to compete with the traditional coal lights then in use, and used his considerable reputation to promote them widely. He convinced the newly founded Northern Lighthouse Board of his lighting expertise, and that his oil lamps were viable in lighthouses. The board had been trying, without success, to recruit an English lighthouse engineer, Ezekiel Walker, of King's Lynn, Norfolk, to assist their building program. He declined to work for them, but offered to build a lighthouse, assist with directions for three more, and "instruct a representative on the whole of the principles and improvements for a fee of 50 guineas." The board took him up only on the last part of his offer, and placed their confidence in Thomas Smith. He traveled almost immediately to meet Walker and gain the knowledge he needed to build and equip the proposed lighthouses around the Scottish coasts. Over the next 20 years he provided the equipment for 13 lighthouses, including one converted from a castle on Kinnaird Head. The castle still has its light, and is now the home of the Scottish Lighthouse Museum.

Robert Stevenson had grown up in this successful atmosphere and eventually went to work installing the lights for the harbor at Portpatrick, Scotland, and was entrusted by his stepfather with installing the light at the Cloch Lighthouse on the Clyde. Although officially still an apprentice, he was the firm's lighthouse specialist. In the last year of the century Robert worked on his proposal to put a light on the infamous Bell Rock in the entrance to the Firth of Forth in the east of Scotland.

Bell Rock Lighthouse, which the young Robert subsequently built, was to test his resolve and competence many times. He abandoned his original scheme for a light on cast-iron pillars as not strong enough. He was almost certainly influenced by John Smeaton's stone tower at Eddystone Lighthouse, which had been built 40 years earlier and was by then well tested by wave action. He took the advice of John Rennie, one of the leading civil engineers of the day, who agreed that the stone tower would be preferred.

During the building, Robert was appointed engineer, the chief executive position, of the Northern Lighthouse Board. During his 35-year tenure he laid down the structure of the modern lighthouse service and was responsible for the design of 23 lighthouses and the improvement of five of the early ones.

The Stevenson dynasty was now well established and set to continue. Alan, the eldest surviving son, was quite firm in his choice of the family business as his career. He was formally apprenticed to his father while a teenager, but became best known for the building of Skerryvore lighthouse off the West Coast of Scotland and for his work on lenses. He extended the firm's influence beyond Scotland when he designed and supervised the installation of the first dioptric lens at Start Point Lighthouse on England's South Devon coast.

BELOW *The English painter J.M.W. Turner captures the terrible weather endured by lighthouse builders and keepers at the Eddystone reef off southwest England.*

EDDYSTONE LIGHTHOUSE

One of the most famous lighthouses in the world stands on the notorious Eddystone Rocks southwest of Plymouth on the south coast of England. It has had several incarnations since the first was lit at the end of the seventeenth century.

The reef's rocks of red granite were considered to be one of the greatest hazards to sailors of the English coasts. Henry Winstanley, a ship owner who had lost three cargoes off the reef, built the first lighthouse there, which was lit in November 1698. However, Winstanley had to rebuild the tower after that first winter's storm waves had gone right over the top of the 80-foot (24-meter) tower and eroded the base.

That second tower, built in 1699, was destroyed in the Great Storm of 1703, and the third lighthouse was built in 1706 by John Rudyerd (a Cornishman who eventually became a successful silk merchant, although little else is known of him), but it was destroyed by fire in 1755. In 1759, the next tower, built by John Smeaton, began operations, and remained until 1882, when it was dismantled owing to erosion and taken ashore, and a replacement was erected by James Douglass in 1882. That tower remains today.

RIGHT *The Eddystone lighthouse stands beside the stump of the previous lighthouse.*

FAR RIGHT TOP *Cross-sections of Eddystone Lighthouse.*

FAR RIGHT BOTTOM *Elevation of Eddystone Rock foundations.*

ABOVE *Laying the foundation stone of Eddystone Lighthouse in 1879.*

BELOW *The five lighthouses that have stood on Eddystone reef.*

Winstanley, 1698

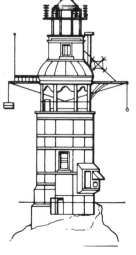

Winstanley, 1699

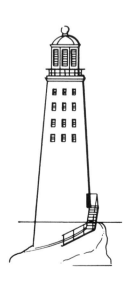

Rudyerd, 1709

Smeaton, 1759

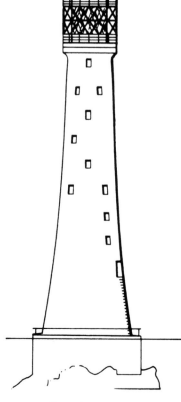

Douglass, 1882

The EDDYSTONE in the 18th CENTURY

RUDYERD 1706

LAMINATED TIMBER

MASONRY

OAK PLANK SHEATHING

IRON ANCHORS

SMEATON 1756

IRON CHAINS EMBEDDED IN LEAD

MARBLE DOWELS

THE WORLD'S LIGHTHOUSES BEFORE 1820

D. ALAN STEVENSON

LONDON
OXFORD UNIVERSITY PRESS
NEW YORK   TORONTO
1959

ABOVE *Imprint page of D. Alan Stevenson's book* The World's Lighthouses Before 1820 *published by Oxford University Press in 1959.*

His younger brothers, David and Thomas, eventually joined him in the business. David was to become known for his detailed engineering work and Thomas for his technical books and professional papers. During the late 1800s the firm built docks in England and lighthouses in Newfoundland, Japan, and many far-flung places, and developed expertise in the control of rivers: building flood banks and performing other river-related maintenance tasks.

David's organizational skills managed the building of Muckle Flugga Lighthouse on an offshore rock to the north of Scotland in just six months. The short time scale for the project was required by the British Admiralty, because Crimea War convoys were sailing round the north of Scotland and the rock was directly in their path. The Stevensons seemed to have influence on many civil engineering projects. In the 1870s the general acceptance of what was then a new fuel, paraffin, in lighthouse illumination owed a great deal to David's work, proving its technical and economic value.

Thomas Stevenson, the inventor (and father of the literary Robert Louis), concerned himself with improving surveying equipment, inventing a wave-measuring device, and investigating the design of cofferdams (walled structures used to create a dry working area in a space otherwise covered by water). He contributed articles to the *Encyclopaedia Britannica* and wrote a textbook called *Lighthouse Illumination*. He was responsible for the lighthouse at Dhu Heartach in the Hebrides, taking with him his 15-year-old nephew, David Alan, who, with his brother Charles, was to provide the fourth generation.

Arguably the most famous Stevenson, Robert Louis (1850–94), author of literary classics such as *Treasure Island* and *Dr. Jekyll and Mr. Hyde* found the family business boring and, though he found the engineering subjects difficult, he managed to write some essays about the subject. For a paper, "A New Form of Intermittent Light for Lighthouses," given to the Royal Scottish Society of Arts in March 1871, he won a silver medal. He obviously had some of the family talent for lighthouse engineering, but, much to the exasperation of his father, he decided against an engineering career.

Lighthouses were still part of the company business, but, by the time David Alan and Charles were trained, the majority of the world's major lighthouses had been erected. David was in 1938 the last Stevenson to hold the post of chief engineer to the Northern Lighthouse Board.

D. Alan Stevenson, the last of the line of the lighthouse Stevensons, concerned himself with the lighthouses of the Indian subcontinent and also worked on improvements to the River Clyde to allow the super-sized transatlantic liners being built to sail when completed. He published a number of books and papers, including the classic work *The World's Lighthouses Before 1820*.

LIGHTHOUSE FAMILIES

Though it may seem that the Stevensons dominated lighthouse engineering in the United Kingdom, we must not overlook sterling work done by others: the Halpins, for instance. In contrast to the publicity that surrounded the Stevensons, little is known about this father-and-son team, both called George. They built more than 50 Irish lighthouses during a 50-year period that started when George Snr. was appointed engineer to the Port of Dublin in about 1810. His first task was to report on the condition of the existing Irish structures, but his own first lighthouse was built on Inishtrahull island in 1812. He followed this with the lighthouse at the entrance to Dublin known as Howth Baily. George Jnr. joined him as his assistant in 1830, finally taking over as the port's engineer in 1849, by which time the majority of the lights attributed to them had been built. George Jnr. was responsible for the first lighthouse built on the Fastnet Rock. It was known as Ireland's Teardrop, because for many of the Irish people emigrating to North America it was their last sight of their home country. By 1860 both father and son were dead.

On the other side of the Irish Sea, their contemporaries were Jesse and John Hartley, father and son respectively, who successively held the post of engineer to the Mersey Docks and Harbour Board. Jesse supervised the building of the lighthouses at Crosby in the northwest of England and Point Lynas on the Welsh island of Anglesey. His unusual design for the latter lighthouse placed the lantern tower at ground level so that the light would be less obscured by fog forming on the surrounding cliffs. John succeeded his father as engineer to the authority, but is known to have built only one lighthouse, the ornate little Plover Scar at the entrance to the River Lune.

By contrast, the Douglass family's interest in lighthouses began when Nicholas Douglass joined Trinity House in 1839 at the relatively advanced age of 41. He was a constructional engineer who worked on the cast-iron lighthouse that was being erected on the Bishop Rock, off the Isles of Scilly. He was joined on this job by his eldest son James, who also worked with him on its stone

ABOVE *Robert Stevenson.*

BELOW *The most northerly lighthouse in the UK, Muckle Flugga.*

rising from having to pass ... the ...

"present door will be avoided."

Fastnet Rock bearing E by S

ABOVE *A drawing of the first lighthouse on Fastnet Rock.*

replacement after the original tower had collapsed. He was to get to know the Bishop Rock site well, for, during his subsequent appointment as the engineer-in-chief for Trinity House, he was forced to reconstruct the lighthouse, which had become unstable through wave action. James's younger brother, William, also worked for Trinity House, in his case for more than 25 years, before becoming the chief engineer to the Commissioners of Irish Lights, a post he held for 20 years. He designed the second tower to be placed on the Fastnet Rock after a survey revealed that the original tower was unsafe. Sir James also had a son, William, working with him. In 1878 William was with his father on the Eddystone, and later became the resident engineer during the strengthening of the Bishop Rock tower and the building of the lighthouse on the nearby Round Island. William was involved in a freak accident on the Eddystone. While he was inspecting the outside of the tower, the a supporting chain failed, caused him to fall nearly 70 feet (21 meters). He was saved from death by a huge wave which caught his body and swept him away from the base rocks so that he could be rescued from the sea.

SOLO BUILDERS

While the lighthouse-building families take their rightful place in this story, most creators of these fascinating structures were individuals. James Walker,

born in Glasgow in 1781, designed and erected 29 towers during his lifetime. Although his first iron tower at the Bishop Rock was not successful, because it was too weak, he became an innovative designer. He used the concept of a stepped base on wave-girt towers to break up the waves and prevent the sea sweeping up the main tower. His attention to detail also included the welfare of the keepers: if space was available he allowed for sheltered courtyards and was the first to build water closets on rock lighthouses.

Other lighthouse engineers became so because of the job they were in. Some were civil servants, such as a Mr. Henderson, who was the first engineer to be appointed by the Chinese Marine Department of Customs. Between 1869 and his retirement in 1898, he was the driving force behind the building of 28 lighthouses in Chinese waters. Some became lighthouse engineers in spite of physical handicaps that would have kept most people safely on shore. Alexander Mitchell, (see Chapter 2) who invented the screw-pile method of building lighthouse on soft sand, was blind from

RIGHT *Fastnet Rock Lighthouse, also known as Ireland's teardrop, so called as it was the last sight of Ireland for emigrants leaving for the New World.*

FAR RIGHT *Cross-section of the earlier Fastnet Rock Lighthouse.*

NEXT PAGE *Bodie Island Lighthouse, N. Carolina, U.S.A.*

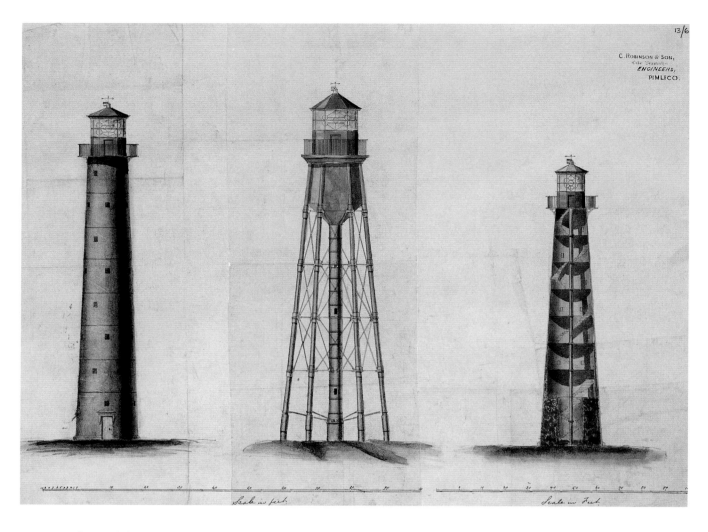

ABOVE *Three lighthouse designs from the 1850s by Robinson and Sons of Pimlico, London.*

birth and Gustaf Dalen, the Swedish inventor was blinded in the middle of his career in 1912, when an experiment using gas went wrong and exploded in his face. The accident delayed the ceremony at which he was to receive the Nobel prize for physics. From the time of his recovery until his death in 1937 at the age of 68, he continued with his inventions and held over 100 patents for innovations ranging from milking machines to radio beacons.

The remit of the European designers and builders did not extend to North America, though some of their ideas undoubtedly did. The early Colonial lights were erected and paid for by the individual Colonial administrations. They used local contractors, who gained the work more by political influence than lighthouse-building and design skills. After the War of Independence, lighthouse building became a federal remit and the President himself was the authority, which was bestowed on him by an Act of Congress dated August 7 1789. The control of the new nation's lighthouses was placed under the U.S. Treasury, where it remained until 1903, when the Lighthouse Board was transferred to the Department of Commerce during a

realignment of responsibilities. The Department of Commerce then, in 1910, reorganized the Lighthouse Board into the Bureau of Lighthouses, under whose control they remained until 1939, when the Presidential Reorganization Act placed them in the control of the US Coast Guard, where they remain today.

In 1799, Henry Dearborn was contracted to build two lighthouses, at Ocracoke inlet and Cape Hatteras, both in North Carolina. He had been a Congressman, ambassador to Portugal, Secretary for War, and a Boston customs collector, and even held the rank of major general in the U.S. Army. His lighthouse at Ocracoke lasted only 20 years before it was destroyed by lightning, but the Cape Hatteras tower was still strong enough in 1854 for the Lighthouse Board to recommend that it be raised from its original height of 95 feet (29 meters) to 150 feet (46 meters) and be fitted with a French-made Fresnel lens. The lighthouse survived until 1867, when it was deemed beyond repair and the present lighthouse was built nearby to replace it.

RIGHT *Ocracoke Island Lighthouse, on the outer banks of North Carolina, was built in 1823 using bricks with a mortar surface.*

Dearborn used English stone and bricks to construct his lighthouse. Whether his methods and design were influenced by English practice is not recorded, though his work coincides with that of Robert Stevenson and he must have known of the lighthouse works of John Smeaton. The town of Dearborn, Michigan (birthplace of Henry Ford), is named after Henry Dearborn, for his services to the nation.

The use of building contractors continued in the United States, and, even with the presence of a government officer on site during the building, many lighthouses were constructed to a poor standard. The names of many builders are lost in obscurity, the works of the better ones remaining as their memorials: Isaac Conro's at Sandy Hook, for example, John McComb Jnr.'s at Cape Henry, and lighthouses built by Alexander Parris of Boston on the Maine coast. Generally, however, the reports of lighthouse inspectors before 1850 are less than complimentary. Many of the 200 or so lighthouses then in commission were in poor condition.

The U.S. was well behind the rest of the world in lighthouse technology. Most of this problem can be laid at the door of the Treasury's Fifth Auditor, Stephen Pleasanton. He was an accountant, not an engineer, which was very apparent during his 32–year tenure. He was much more concerned with controlling expenditure than providing efficient and quality lighthouses. This parsimony held sway, so much so that from 1810 the lighting equipment specified by the Fifth Auditor was supplied by one single contractor.

Captain Winslow Lewis, an unemployed ship's master, had gained some lighthouse engineering knowledge during voyages to Europe. This he used to "develop" an Argand lamp for the U.S. market. In 1810 after some years of experiment and a public exhibition of his "new" light at the Boston Lighthouse, his design was accepted. His quality was poor but his prices were always accepted by Pleasanton. This did not change for many years, and nor did the lack of approval to spend money to obtain the better European optics of the Fresnel type. Complaints by ship owners, pilots, and mariners forced the U.S. government to set up an inquiry into the condition of the country's lighthouse stock.

The inquiry board's report confirmed the complaints and in 1851 a new Lighthouse Board was set up by an Act of Congress. It comprised two naval officers, two army engineers, a civilian scientist, and a naval secretary. The new board had a large remit and set about reorganizing the building, equipping, and maintenance of the country's lighthouses. The immediate effect was the introduction of French-made Fresnel lens systems, the repair of buildings, and the training of keepers. The board

remained in existence until 1910, when it was superceded by a less military-based Bureau of Lighthouses led by George Putnam, a nonmilitary man with an engineering background. He controlled and developed the United States Lighthouse Service as a civilian organization until he retired in 1936. The U.S. Lighthouse Service was merged into the U.S. Coastguard in 1939, under whose jurisdiction it remains today.

THE COURAGEOUS MR. BALLANTYNE

While the United States did not build many tall rock towers, or have its lighthouses built by household names, there were many unsung heroes and many dedicated men. Some were high-ranking officials, others merely men employed to build a lighthouse. George Ballantyne was one of the latter, and his story of the building of Tillamook lighthouse off the coast of Oregon will serve as testimony for them all.

Ballantyne was a mason foreman working for the U.S. Lighthouse Board in the latter part of the nineteenth century. His building site was a lump of sheer-sided black basalt a mile offshore and in the path of ferocious storms. The storms, the sandbar at the Columbia River entrance, and the rocks of Tillamook Head claimed the lives of many ships' crews and accelerated the demands by the people of Oregon for a lighthouse to mark the entrance to the Columbia River.

The initial surveys looked to place a lighthouse on the cliffs on the southern side of the entrance. Though it was an ideal place, the surveyors thought it was too inaccessible, many of the cliffs on this coast reaching up to 1,640 feet (500 meters) high. So any lighthouse erected would be lost in the frequent low cloud and fog. The Tillamook Rock, about 20 miles further south, was finally chosen after much deliberation.

Though public opinion demanded a lighthouse, many in the small ports on the Columbia River thought the choice of Tillamook Rock was too dangerous, and that the project would be completed only at the cost of human life. The inaccessibility of the site led to incessant delays in the surveying, and pressure on the surveyors from the Lighthouse Board steeled one of the more experienced men, an Englishman, John Trewavas, who was determined to get on the rock at all costs. Although he was an experienced surveyor, having worked on the Wolf Rock, in the tides and storms of the English Channel, Tillamook Rock was his downfall, for, during an attempt to land, he was cast down by a huge roller and swept away.

In spite of these setbacks, the Lighthouse Board was determined to get work well under way before the tide of public opinion turned against the work.

ABOVE *Tillamook Lighthouse, Oregon, U.S.A.*

It was in this sorry atmosphere that Ballantyne and eight highly skilled quarrymen arrived at Astoria, the nearest embarkation point, to set up a base at the end of September 1879. He was assured that his supplies and accommodation for his men would be waiting for him on his arrival so that work could start immediately. But his superiors had forgotten, or had chosen to ignore the weather! The autumnal gales had already set in, making it impossible to get to and land on the rock.

Ballantyne was concerned that his men would become demoralized by tavern gossip and abandon the job, so he rushed his men away from the town to spare keeper's quarters some miles away at Cape Disappointment Lighthouse. After 26 days of enforced idleness, they at last could make a move toward the rock. By superb seamanship and with much difficulty, four men and their tools were put on the rock. The weather blew up quickly and the four were left to their own devices as the cutter sailed for safety.

Five days later, a window in the weather allowed the cutter to return and land the remainder of the party and more equipment. The only "shelter" was provided by sleeping blankets, so to get out of the relentless and brutal wind they burrowed into rock fissures and any other places that they could find.

As soon as the workforce were established, a derrick with a long arm was rigged so that men and supplies could be lifted directly off the supply ship waiting below. To form a level site the fissured top of the rock was drilled and blasted to remove more than 20 feet (6 meters) of rock until a smooth surface was gained. Even this high above

the waves, spray would soak the gunpowder and prevent it firing, and men would be cold and wet. They also sometimes had to rope themselves to pitons to stop themselves falling off the rock as they worked. During all this, Ballantyne was a tower of strength, cajoling, threatening, and, by example, pushing the job forward. He wanted to erect permanent quarters for them all as soon as possible, because they were living in atrocious conditions with only canvas tents for protection.

His actions came just in time. The new year of 1880 greeted them with the ultimate test. Over a period of six days winds built up hurricane force, culminating in a tornado with Tillamook Rock at its center. By midnight on January 6, with the storm still increasing, the frightened men huddled in their new permanent quarters listening to rocks crashing down on the roof. In the morning they discovered their store shed had been destroyed. They had lost most of their provisions, including the freshwater tank. They had to wait another 10 days before the cutter could leave the safety of Astoria to see if they were safe. The cutter managed to land some supplies before the weather intervened again. It was the end of January before the construction supply ship managed to get near the derrick to allow a proper transfer of badly needed stores and extra men. However, even during the time they were cut off, Ballantyne saw that work was carried out as and when the weather allowed.

Ballantyne's tenacity and determination were rewarded: as winter retreated he was able to make the work progress, while ashore public opinion was turning in favor of this extraordinary band of courageous men, who, without further loss of life, were able to complete the lighthouse by January

21, 1881, when they exhibited the light for the first time. Before this, the workmen had warned ships away in fog by exploding charges when they heard the vessels' fog signals. They saved a number of ships, who steered away from danger in the nick of time. Mariners showed their appreciation of the efforts of Ballantyne and his men by sailing close to the rock when they were on passage passing to look for signals in case assistance was needed.

Tillamook Rock lighthouse was one of the most difficult jobs tackled by the Lighthouse Board. The men had worked for nearly 600 days to put the light, fog signal, and keepers' quarters in place.

BUILDERS WITH CONVICTIONS . . .

One of the first beacons in Australia, a coal-burning tower, was built in 1805 at Coal River, New South Wales. While searching for escaped convicts in 1797, Lieutenant John Shortland of the Royal Navy had discovered coal and started a settlement. It is not known whether he found the escapees or whether convicts actually built the tower.

The architect who set the style for many New South Wales lighthouses, however, was definitely a convict. Francis Howard Greenway had been transported from his native Bristol in southwest England after a death sentence was commuted to transportation to the penal colony of New South Wales. This did not stop the young architect from finding favor with Governor Lachlan Macquarie soon after his arrival in Sydney. Macquarie was the first military governor, his predecessors all being naval officers, though none had bothered with lighthouses.

Macquarie instituted a program of public works, using Greenway as his architect. One of his first buildings was a lighthouse he erected on the south head of Sydney Harbour. The 75–foot (23–meter) tower was constructed of a soft local sandstone and built by convict labor. The light was a revolving triangular frame holding three oil-fired lamps with reflectors made in Sydney by Robinson and Company. Though the lighthouse was a success, Macquarie gained official displeasure for spending public money without London's approval. The light was shown for the first time on November 30, 1818, and became known as Macquarie Lighthouse. Greenway died in poverty in 1837, but his lighthouse designs lived on and were adopted in 15 lighthouses in New South Wales, including two on offshore islands.

While most lighthouse sites could be gained from the sea, there were others where the assigned spot for a new building was accessible only by land. Cape Otway on the Australian shore of the infamous Bass Strait is one well-documented story of the trials and tribulations that faced the early surveyors.

The Bass Strait was the graveyard of a large number of sailing ships, but the fact that many were convict ships (and by definition did not seem to matter) did not stir the authorities to action. It was the loss of the *Cataraqui* and 414 emigrants on August 4, 1845, and the subsequent publicity, that finally galvanized the authorities.

The ramifications of the disaster spread as far as the House of Commons in London, where Members of Parliament called for the Bass Strait lighthouse to be built. But, even before orders had been issued, the superintendent of the Port Philip district of New South Wales, Charles La Trobe, had pre-empted them. La Trobe was a man of action. He had interviewed some of the survivors, made arrangements for the burial of the dead, and, without awaiting instruction, set out to explore a land route to the distant Cape Otway. The area was inhospitable subtropical

BELOW *The twin lights of Thatcher Island, one of the few twin-tower stations originally constructed in 1789.*

rainforest, cut by rivers and mountain ranges. La Trobe set out within a month of the disaster, at his own expense and with the knowledge that two explorers, Gellibrand and Hess, had been lost without trace in 1837.

La Trobe, accompanied by two Aborigine police troopers, Bluebeard and Noggy, had set out with a mounted trooper to find settlers who could help him. He failed, noting in his diary: "Try for Hamilton's and get entangled in forest and creek. Heavy rain … Chilled and unwell …" His party returned home. With pressure mounting from Sydney, he knew he must try again. This he did in December, but from the opposite direction, accompanied by Superintendent Henry Dana with his troop of Native Police Aborigine. The party eventually linked up with a settler, Henry Allan (who, with his brother, owned the Allansford station, now a small town), who loaned La Trobe one of his Aborigine trackers. Once again, weather, terrain, and ill heath forced a despondent return.

The Colonial Secretary and Colonial Architect, both sitting safely in Sydney, needed information to allow them to be seen to be taking action and continued the pressure on La Trobe to get to the proposed site. La Trobe set out again in March 1846 with his faithful policemen and helped by Henry Allen. With every confidence the party expected to get to Cape Otway. They forded creeks, cut pathways through forest, were cold, wet, and exhausted most of the time, but La Trobe was finally to record in his diary: "Push forward and reach the highest sand hill … and know that we have really found Cape Otway …" Though he had found his site, he knew that the route would be impossible for contractors and their bullock carts.

La Trobe returned home, from where, in a letter to the Colonial Secretary in Sydney, he gave details of the area

ABOVE *The Macquarie Lighthouse, Sydney, Australia, was built in 1817. The illustration by Sainson shows it as it was in 1830.*

proposed for the lighthouse. He commissioned Henry Allen to find a suitable route for a trail and arranged for a government surveyor to conduct a coastal survey. Henry Allen failed to find the trail and the government surveyor, William Smythe, lost a man, who was murdered by the Aborigines, and caused a massacre when retaliating. However, the survey was completed and a trail blazed by the father and son, William and Thomas Roadknight.

The Roadknights were grazers and had heard about the potential grazing in the Otway ranges. They pushed a 65-mile trail suitable for bullock carts and cattle from their cattle station to Cape Otway. A surprised La Trobe received the information in a letter from Roadknight Snr. dated August 25, 1846: "I have succeeded in completing a track thereto …" He went on to describe the track and the problems they had encountered. Roadknight's reward was a grazing station in virgin country, and La Trobe was able to report progress. The designs were finished and the lighthouse built, its lantern, made in London, delivered by sea through the surf into a creek that the surveyor Smythe had discovered. The light was first exhibited on the evening of November 30, 1848.

These stories tell of the hardships and adversity that had to be overcome to build lighthouses. This was just the start of the story. All the major lighthouses were looked after by keepers, sometimes two or three men on an isolated rock station, sometimes with the companionship and assistance of their families on remote islands, while the fortunate few were part of small townships.

Chapter 5 | LIGHTHOUSE LORE

Lighthouse keeping has never been a job for an excitable person with a nervous disposition. One attribute of paramount importance was to be able to take life as it came; another was to be able to tolerate one's fellow man. Even on land stations with the company of families, keepers' very survival relied on helping each other through emotional times. On the offshore lighthouses, two or three men lived a bachelor existence, cheek by jowl for their month-long shifts, when minor idiosyncrasies and foibles that might be ignored ashore could cause major conflict in their confined environment.

FAMILIES WERE OFTEN CLOSELY involved in lighthouse keeping. If the lighthouse was offshore, the family would be housed in a cottage provided by the lighthouse authority, usually in a small community of other keepers. On island and land stations the families could live at the lighthouse, though with school-age children this sometimes forced keepers to send their families to lodge in the nearest town. Teresa Ball lived in her lighthouse keeper's cottage at Hugh Town on St. Mary's, one of the Isles of Scilly southwest of England. Her husband, John, was the principal keeper on the Bishop Rock Lighthouse just half an hour's boat trip away. On December 19, 1898, Teresa had left her home to go to the mainland to look after her daughter-in-law, Mary-Ann, and Mary-Ann's new baby, Aubrey. Sadly, on that day her husband went missing in strange circumstances. He was accustomed on calm days to go outside onto the lighthouse landing to enjoy a pipe of tobacco, which he did on the fateful day. His fellow keepers became worried when he did not return to the mess room, as normal. Although

weather conditions were good, he had vanished! Teresa was not told of the disappearance until her return some days later. She was sure that he would turn up, for John was a reliable husband and a caring father. Every day for some weeks she sent her children, Charles and Edmund, to the beach in the hope that either they would find her husband safe or, as the days went by, his body would come ashore so that he could have a Christian burial. He was never found, and the mystery was never solved. Charles and Edmund, and the baby Aubrey, were in time all to become lighthouse keepers, not put off by the tragedy.

AND BABY CAME, TOO . . .

The loss of keepers or members of their families was not an unusual occurrence. For mothers there was always the fear that the children would fall over cliffs. Lighthouse children

RIGHT *An idyllic view of a lighthouse keeper's life from the cover of the Saturday Evening Post magazine, June 26, 1954.*

adapted quickly to their environment, enjoying the lighthouse as an adventure playground without equal. One mother, Betty Strowbridge, who lived at a number of lighthouses on the cliffs of Newfoundland in the 1980s, said in a CBC radio interview that "they were like mountain goats." Other mothers used harnesses and lines to ensure the safety of their young.

Many children raised on lighthouses looked back in later years at the happy times that they had. Typical was Norma Engel, who was raised on Ballast Point Lighthouse near San Diego in the 1920s and wrote in her book *Three Beams of Light* in 1986. "I loved going up the tower. From the outside walkway I could look down on the tops of nearby dwellings and see all around …" Her family looked after three lighthouses over a span of 37 years, including a difficult couple of years in temporary accommodation on Point Bonita, California, after the lighthouse and their home were severely damaged during the 1906 San Francisco earthquake.

BELOW *Brass cleaning was a necessary but time-consuming chore for lighthouse keepers. Although keeping the brass clean was a requirement of the job, most keepers took great pride in their brasswork.*

FATHER MARRIES SON!

The Thompson family kept lights in the far-flung corners of the Bahamas for many generations. George Thompson arrived in the islands from England in 1839 and married a local girl from Abaco Island. They raised a number of sons and daughters. When George was the principal keeper of Abaco Lighthouse, the Bahamas government also appointed him registrar of marriages for the district. His eldest son had the unique experience of being married by his own father in his own lighthouse home!

KEEPERS AND DAUGHTERS

Marjorie Congdon grew up on Watch Hill Lighthouse, Rhode Island, in the 1930s. It was a popular place for visitors, so she and her sister, Edna, had no shortage of friends for the social life of teenage girls. One of the visitors was a young carpenter, Clifford Pendleton, who courted her and proposed marriage. At the age of 20, after a marriage service at the lighthouse, she left to become a housewife and mother a few miles away. However, many keepers' daughters stayed to become keepers themselves.

Abigail Burgess was a well known American lighthouse keeper. She learned her trade working with her father, Samuel, at Matinicus Rock Light Station. This lighthouse is about 25 miles off the coast of Maine. Her father, appointed there in 1853, took with him his invalid wife, a son, and four daughters. Abigail was the eldest. She acted as housekeeper and helped her father tend the light. Her brother was away fishing so not able to help. On one occasion, during a major storm in January 1856, when her father was on the mainland getting supplies, this resolute girl not only kept the light burning but saved her family by moving them from the damaged house to the safety of the tower as seas swept the island. The weather prevented her father or brother from returning, so she and her sisters kept the light burning for 4 weeks.

In 1861 her father's tenure was ended, owing to a change in federal government. In those days, most U.S. lighthouse keepers' appointments were political ones. He resigned with good grace but left his daughter to show the new keeper, John Grant, the station. John Grant's son was the assistant and soon fell in love with Abigail. She stayed on, and the following year they married. Although she was more experienced—having worked the lighthouse for nearly 10 years—being a woman meant she could not be given seniority over the men, so she was appointed third assistant keeper. She combined this job with running her family of four both on Matinicus Lighthouse and later at Whitehead Lighthouse, Penobscot Bay, Maine. She died at the relatively early age of 52, probably worn out by a hard life.

ALL IN A DAY'S WORK . . .

Lighthouse keepers did not see themselves as heroes, but just as people doing a job. Sometimes their own lives were put at risk to save others. William Darling and his daughter Grace—keepers of the Longstone Lighthouse on the Farne Islands off the North Sea coast of Northumberland, England—certainly did when they braved the cold stormy waters off the coast in September 1838. In the early hours of the morning they saw the wreck of the paddle steamer *Forfarshire* hard on the rocks near the lighthouse. The ship was on passage from Hull in northern England to Dundee in Scotland with 60 people on board when boiler trouble caused her engine to fail through lack of steam. She attempted to shelter in the lee of the island, but was swept on the shore.

Grace and her father jumped into their boat and rowed to the stricken ship, where they found only nine survivors. While Grace kept the boat away from the rocks, her father placed some of the injured survivors into it, and they then rowed back to the lighthouse. While Grace tended them, her father took two men who were uninjured with him to return to save the remaining people. Grace Darling's part in the rescue fired public imagination, and overshadowed her father's bravery. Her portrait was painted, her story told in plays, and even locks of hair, supposedly from her head, were sold as souvenirs of the incident. Her lighthouse-keeping days were short lived, though, because within four years she had died of tuberculosis.

FROM TOP TO BOTTOM *Grace Darling; William Darling; the couragoeus rescue.*

NOT A WOMAN'S PLACE

The official, rather negative attitude regarding females looking after lighthouses remained until quite recently. A letter written in 1716, by the clerk to the fraternity of Trinity House at Newcastle-upon-Tyne in the north of England to the disabled old keeper at the North Shields lighthouse, Newcastle, sums up the attitude:

> Honest Roger, Be not discouraged that John Dobbins is commanded to take care of the lights. He will be no detriment to you but rather a help; and though your maid be a fine ingenious carefull lass, yet it doth not stand with the honour of the Trinity House to leave so great a charge to the management of a woman. . . .Do not feare but our masters will take care of you as long as you live!

Nothing is known about the "carefull lass," except that she was a young girl who looked after the old man, and tended the candle lamps. Very few lighthouse authorities employed women as keepers, though they were always willing to allow the keepers' wives to be unpaid helpers.

The United States Lighthouse Service was an exception in that it eventually employed women at some lighthouses, sometimes with their daughters as assistants. Ida Lewis, who kept Lime Rock Lighthouse in Newport, Rhode Island, took it over after the death of her father in 1872, though she was not officially accepted in the post till 1879. Ida was to become one of the most famous female keepers. She met President Ulysses Grant, received many lifesaving awards, and was featured in an edition of *Harper's Weekly* after she had carried out a rescue. As recently as 1995, the U.S. Coastguard honored her by naming a new class of buoy tender after her. Ida married a local fisherman, but this lasted only a few months. For the rest of her life, until her late sixties, she looked after her light, and was eventually found dying on the floor of the lantern room having suffered a brain hemorrhage.

ROMANTICS NEED NOT APPLY

Keeping a light was not for the faint-hearted, the idle, or the romantic. Danger lurked at every turn, routine jobs had to be carried out, and practicality took sway over all activities. Yet most keepers or their families would not have changed places for a less eventful occupation. Some wives were assistant keepers; many sons followed their fathers; daughters married keepers. But lighthouse keeping was not for dreamers or those who saw lighthouse keeping as an easy meal ticket. They soon found out that, whether the job offered stability or not, the key features were monotony and loneliness.

Wives and families are an integral piece of the story. When the husband was based on a rock, families worried about his loneliness, the weather conditions he was enduring, and whether his relief might be late in arriving, thus delaying his homecoming. But contrasting with this woe was the joy of regular reunions. On a land station, often isolated, family life revolved round the lighthouse: without fail the light had to be "put in" (lit) at sunset and tended during the night. The whole gamut of human emotion and experience was encountered looking after a lighthouse.

LEFT *Abigail Burgess tending her light at Matinicus Rock Light Station during her father's absence. Wives and daughters of keepers were often called upon to stand in during the keeper's absence ashore, such as when fetching stores, to ensure that the light was kept on. The work was just as hard for them but, with a few exceptions, it was unpaid and rarely acknowledged.*

RIGHT *This lonely lighthouse perched on its rock off the Irish Coast is appropriately named the Black Rock Lighthouse. The photographer, approaching by helicopter, has captured the loneliness of such isolated lighthouses.*

LIGHTHOUSE INTERIORS

Living quarters, especially in offshore tower lighthouses, were cramped. The tower had to contain not only the keeper's living area but also all the storage and operating equipment. The spiral staircase dominated each floor level leaving little room for privacy. The keepers only privacy was when they were in their curved, banana-shaped bunks when they could draw the curtain accross.

LEFT *A scene from the 1850s (taken from the Strand Magazine) of the keepers relaxing at one of the British offshore lighhouses, probably Eddystone.*

BELOW *The kitchen at Beachy Head Lighthouse taken in the 1980s prior to the station becoming automatic. The fact that the window is open indicates that it is an unusually calm day.*

RIGHT *The spotless staircase at Ile Vierge, France, highlights the tedious chore that cleaning must have been.*

MURDER MOST FOUL

Murder may have often been in the hearts of men closeted together for weeks, but thankfully irritation rarely erupted beyond mere arguments. Keepers knew the risks involved and tended to bottle up aggression. Most stations' duty turns passed without incident, with keepers getting on with the job in harmony. However, for Hugh Clark and George Dickson, keepers of Little Ross Island Lighthouse on the Solway Firth, between northwestern England and southern Scotland, a duty spell during the summer of 1960 ended in a death and a suicide. Hugh Clark was killed with a sawn-off shotgun by his assistant; the reason for the incident was never known, for George Dickson escaped from the island and fled more than 200 miles to Selby in Yorkshire, where he committed suicide. Clark's body was found during a visit by two people who had sailed to the island for a picnic. They decided to call at the lighthouse while on the island, but at first they could not find any keepers, so returned to the jetty to have their picnic. Afterwards, just before leaving, they decided to return to the lighthouse. On this second visit they found the door of one of the keepers' cottages swinging open, and, on entering and searching the rooms, discovered the murdered keeper's body in one of the bedrooms.

DEATH AND MADNESS

Little Ross Lighthouse was unusual in having just two keepers. The majority of isolated stations had a minimum of three. It is said that this resulted from an incident on the Smalls Lighthouse off Pembrokeshire in Wales in the 18th century, when one of the two keepers, Tom Griffiths, died. His fellow keeper, Tom Howells, did not bury the body in the sea because he thought that he would be accused of murder. He placed the body into a cask, which he lashed to the lantern gallery. The keeper carried on with his duties while trying to attract the attention of passing ships. No one saw his signals, and the boatmen bringing his relief some weeks later found him in a terrible state. He had gone mad, and some reports said his hair had turned white! His story was believed and he was pensioned off.

THE MYSTERY OF THE MISSING KEEPERS

The lighthouse on the Flannan Islands off the west coast of Scotland was built in 1899 and manned by three keepers whose families all resided on the island of Lewis some

---

MAD HATTER'S DISEASE

Lighthouse keepers are notorious for their wicked sense of humor and practical jokes played to relieve the monotony. Many of the practical jokes, though harmless, are not printable. When asked by visitors to explain how ordinary men could put up with the way of life, they often claimed that madness helped. Yet for some keepers at the end of the nineteenth century it was a real occupational hazard. As the optics became heavier, they were supported in a bath of mercury, which formed a frictionless bearing (see Chapter 3). We now know that mercury must be handled with extreme care, but the early keepers had no such guidance. The effect of mercury spilled on the skin was insidious, because the metal was absorbed only slowly, but eventually led to brain damage. The resulting symptoms were known as the Mad Hatter's disease, so called because it was prevalent in the millinery trade where mercury was used to stiffen felt hats.

distance away. The relief tender, *Hesperus*, collected a relief keeper on Boxing Day, 1900, and sailed for the island on what was to be a routine changeover. On arrival, off the landing jetty, the ship raised the relief flag to warn the keepers to get down from the lighthouse to receive the ship's boat, stores, and relief. When no responding signal was made, the ship first sounded its siren and then fired rockets. When there was still no sign of life, the captain of the tender ordered a boat to take a landing party to the island. They landed safely and searched for the keepers, but could not find them. Further detailed searches revealed that the light was in order and working, but the clocks and log entries had stopped a week before. The station was in good order with the kitchen clean, meal cleared away, and all beds made. There was nothing to suggest foul play or accident. The party did find some damage at the landing jetty, though: a one-ton block of stone had crashed down, some hand railings were damaged, and some of the ropes and equipment missing. The island was again thoroughly searched but no further evidence was found. There was much conjecture in the national press, plus scandalous rumor about the incident concerning a clandestine affair and a fatal fist fight. The official inquiry by a member of the Northern Lighthouse Board concluded that the most likely cause was that the three keepers had for some unexplained reason gone down to the landing and were washed away by a freak wave.

IN TIMES OF WAR

Lighthouses and keepers have always suffered in times of war, and surprisingly not always by enemy action. Warring factions often razed the early lighthouses, which, because they were an aid to navigation, were always in the front line. A band of Seminole Indians attacked the Cape Florida Lighthouse, situated at the northern end of Biscayne Bay. Fearing Indian attack, the keeper, James Dubose, and his family had decamped to Key West, leaving the assistant, John Thompson, with an old Negro hired hand called Aaron Carter, to keep the light. On the evening of July 23, 1836, the band of Indians attacked. Just in time, Thompson and Carter managed to lock themselves in the tower. The enraged attackers peppered the tower with musket balls and set fire to the door in an attempt to get to the pair. Oil from cans knocked over by the keepers in their haste to climb the tower, and pieced by shot, soaked Thompson and helped the fire to spread up the tower. Gaining hold, it forced the two men up the tower and out on to the gallery. Thompson, though burned and hurt, returned fire. A musket bullet

RIGHT *The current Smalls Lighthouse, Wales.*

killed his helper, and the unfortunate keeper was almost roasted alive. He tried to end his agony by throwing a keg of gunpowder into the flames, hoping to blow up the tower and himself, but failed. Later, while trying throw himself off the gallery, he saw a U.S. Navy vessel approaching his jetty. The tower was a burned-out shell, and he had no way of climbing down, so waited for help to arrive. His rescuers tried unsuccessfully to lift him from the gallery with the aid of a kite. While man-carrying kites were used for military observation, it's likely that this would have been used to try to get a line over the tower, so that a jackstay could be rigged for him to climb down. Eventually, they managed to *shoot* a line over the gallery rail. Thompson managed to grab this and hoist up a rope and pulley block, which he made fast to the railing. Two sailors were hauled up to him and were able to lower him to safety. The lighthouse was rebuilt but continual harassment by the Indians delayed the relighting until 1846. Thompson did not return to light keeping.

During the two World Wars lighthouses continued to be manned. Some were armed but on many the keepers were left to fend for themselves, putting the light in (the technical term for lighting the lamp) to aid passing convoys when instructed by the military authorities. Combatants usually respected the lighthouses, reasoning that they were useful marks for them to use on enemy coasts. Sometimes lighthouses were attacked for no reason.

The South Lighthouse on Fair Isle off the northwest coast of Scotland was on the flight path of German planes en route to attack convoys in the North Atlantic. In spite of long periods of darkness, the lighthouse was attacked on a number of occasions. During the first incident in December 1941 a stray bullet killed 22-year-old Catherine Sutherland, the assistant keeper's wife, but left his two-year-old daughter unharmed at the side of her dead mother. The second attack a few days later passed without injury to keepers or their families. In January 1942, the lighthouse was bombed.

Though the tower was not damaged, the building housing the three keepers and their families received a direct hit. The assistant keeper, George Craigie, was

BELOW *Painting from Trinity House of LV 72 on station on Juno Beach in June 1944. It marked the clear passage through the enemy minefields for the ships of the Allied Nations.*

trapped for a short time by a fallen ceiling but managed to extricate himself. Willi Smith, the principal keeper, who witnessed the attack while walking back to the lighthouse from the post office, found his wife Margaret, his 10–year-old daughter Greta, and a visiting soldier, William Morris, fatally injured in the remains of their quarters. The bomb had exploded in the cellar below the houses, igniting the coal stocks, which burned for a week. The light, kept in action by the survivors, aided by the assistant from the North Lighthouse, who trudged daily three miles through snowdrifts and gales to help. Britain's Princess Royal, Princess Anne, unveiled a plaque to the memory of the four victims during a visit in 1998.

Belle Tout Lighthouse on the cliff top at Beachy Head in southeastern England was built in 1828 but abandoned by Trinity House in 1899, owing to stability problems, and replaced by a temporary lightship until the new lighthouse was built at the base of the cliff. During World War I it remained undamaged. And, in spite of further landslides, the lighthouse did not fall down and was used in succeeding years as a family home. During World War II its tower was used as a target by gunners practicing at a nearby range. It was not entirely destroyed and after the war it was rebuilt to serve again as a family home and as the location for a television film. Further recent cliff erosion put the lighthouse in grave danger of falling into the sea. Contractors painstakingly moved it 50 feet (15 meters) away from the edge in March 1999.

The Matagorda Lighthouse

The Matagorda Lighthouse was first lit on December 31, 1852.

During the Civil War, Confederate Forces partially destroyed the lighthouse. In 1873, the Lighthouse was rebuilt two miles to the southwest at its present location to a height of 92 feet.

It was the oldest operating lighthouse on the Texas Coast when the light was dismantled in 1995.

The Matagorda Island Lighthouse is listed on the National Register of Historic Places.

ABOVE *Matagorda Lighthouse, Texas, U.S.A.*

During the Civil War, many American lighthouses suffered from the guns of both sides. Mobile Point Lighthouse, Alabama, was shelled by the Union Navy, reducing it to a ruin, during a bombardment of the nearby Fort Morgan in 1864, and it was never rebuilt. Its near neighbor, the Sand Island Lighthouse, was blown up by the opposing Confederate Army in the same year, but was important enough to be rebuilt and today remains the only coastal lighthouse on the Alabama shoreline.

STORMY WEATHER

Fierce storms were part of a keeper's way of life and, unless they were particularly damaging, they were merely noted as wind force and direction in his log. For one of the greatest storms of all time we must go back to the so-called "Great Storm" of 1703 (which we touched on in Chapter 1). This originated as a Caribbean hurricane, but, instead of losing its power on its track across the Atlantic, arrived on British shores, bringing ferocious winds of destruction. As it crossed southern England, it swept away homes, wrecked hundreds of ships, some still in harbor, and blew away over 400 windmills. Its trail of devastation included the Eddystone Lighthouse off Plymouth. Its builder, Henry Winstanley, was one of the victims. He had sailed out to the lighthouse with a repair crew as soon as the wind had died away after the initial onslaught, only to be caught as the eye of the storm passed over with ever stronger winds following it. The next morning, November 28, 1703, there was no sign of the lighthouse or any of the men on it.

The pile lighthouse on Minot's Ledge off Boston suffered a similar fate during the storms of 1851. The lighthouse was never found, though the bodies of the two keepers were eventually washed ashore. The history of the lighthouses of the Southern states shows that many of them were damaged by storm. The Key West Lighthouse was wrecked in 1846, killing the keeper and his family, whereas the lighthouse at Loggerhead Key was battered badly on many occasions but survived. The Tybee Island Lighthouse at the entrance to the Savannah River still stands today, but the tower suffered more than most. At various times in its history it was damaged by wind, suffered earthquakes, and, as if that were not enough, was purposely destroyed during the Civil War, when the Confederates, in an attempt to thwart the enemy, removed the lens and set fire to the interior.

During a violent thunderstorm on January 21, 1991, at New South Wales's Barranjoey Lighthouse, winds up to Force 17 (143 miles/230 kilometers an hour) forced hailstones almost three inches (70 millimeters) in diameter through the lantern room glazing, which was nearly half an inch (about 10 millimeters) thick. The lighthouse was unmanned and, although the lens was undamaged, the continual lightning strikes blew the main fuses.

An attendant on a routine visit at Christmas 1999 to St. Ann's Head lighthouse on the cliffs of the Welsh coast was surprised to find a large, heavy, circular oil tank embedded in a wall. A storm-force wind had rolled it from one side of the station to the other, a distance of nearly 660 feet (200 meters).

ABOVE *Bird's-eye view of Rotersand Lighthouse, Germany.*

RIGHT *Nividic Lighthouse, Brittany, France, buffeted by wind and waves.*

SHIFTING SANDS

Cape Henlopen Lighthouse on Delaware Bay was built in 1767; it was burned by the British forces during the Revolution and not rebuilt until 1784. The new lighthouse was erected about a mile from the sea on a sandy shore. By 1788, it was noticed that the sand was being swirled away, undermining the base. Bushes were planted in an attempt to control this erosion. Nature then changed her tactics and the opposite happened: sand was piled up against the tower, so much so that new keepers' quarters had to be built, and one of the principal tasks of the keepers was shoveling sand away from the base of the tower. A storm in 1883 caused the sea to reach the tower, risking undermining the foundations. The hull of a ship, wrecked to the north of the tower during the following year, formed a groin that caused the beach to re-form. Lighthouse Board engineers saw that this might be the answer, and employed workmen to build more groins using stone and brushwood. These, however, were washed away almost as quickly as they were built. By 1899 the erosion regime had reversed and the base was once again exposed. Twenty-seven years later, nature won its battle: the tower was toppled in a severe storm on April 13, 1926. There was no loss of life or equipment, though, because the problem of erosion was known and attempts to halt it had been tried, unsuccessfully; so the lighthouse had been abandoned to its fate two years earlier, and all the equipment, including the lens, had been removed.

Cape Hatteras, 260 miles further south on the Outer Banks of North Carolina, had a similar history, but, under a major program in 1999, was moved 960 yards (878 meters) inland to save it from the encroachment by the sea and prevent a loss to North American lighthouse heritage. (We look in more detail at the saving of Hatteras in Chapter 9.)

BELOW *Bugio Lighthouse at the entrance to Lisbon harbor, Portugal.*

RIGHT *Cape Hatteras, North Carolina—always threatened by the encroaching sea.*

BETWEEN A WRECK AND A HARD PLACE

The 2,000-ton sailing ship *Dimsdale* was trying to avoid a submerged wreck when she collided with the well-lit Wonga Shoal pile light near Port Adelaide, South Australia, during a dark winter night in 1907. After the accident, divers investigating the stricken lighthouse found the bodies of the head keeper, Henry Franson, in the lantern tower with severe head bruises and his assistant, Charles McGowan, in the galley with shocking injuries. At the subsequent inquiry into the accident it was decided that both men (who were over 60 years old) had died on impact, not by drowning. The *Dimsdale's* master, Captain John Jones, was familiar with Port Adelaide and the approach past the lighthouse. He steered his ship on a course between the light and the known position of the wreck toward the semaphore anchorage; the crew were taking in sail and preparing to anchor. She refused to respond to the helm and drifted down onto the lighthouse at three and a half knots. The subsequent inquiry found that he had been negligent in approaching too close to the lighthouse and suspended his ticket—his certificate of competency was taken away from him—for 12 months. A manslaughter charge was laid but Jones was acquitted, the jury accepting his defense that he had made a simple miscalculation of distances.

Further along the same coast on June 21, 1976, in foggy conditions, the 7,000-ton cargo ship *Melbourne Trader* collided with the Gellibrand Pile Lighthouse, Port Philip Bay, in the approaches to Melbourne, wrecking both ship and lighthouse. There are no reports that anyone was hurt, but the badly damaged lighthouse could not be economically repaired, and, because it was a danger to navigation, it was destroyed by fire.

BELOW *A painting by Coxwain Lionel Derek Scott, BEM, of the Mumbles Lifeboat, commemorating the loss of a previous lifeboat from the station, in sight of the Mumbles Lighthoue in 1883.*

RIGHT *Ar-men Lighthouse, off the coast of Brittany.*

NEXT PAGE *Waves almost engulf Le Four Lighthouse, Brittany.*

IMMOVABLE OBJECT

A story appears from time to time about a radio-telephone conversation that went as follows:

> "Vessel bearing southwest two miles, this is a U.S. warship. Please alter course. Over."

> The reply was: "U.S. warship, we are on that bearing, but cannot alter course. Over."

> "Vessel bearing southwest two miles, this is U.S. warship. We are an aircraft carrier and order you to alter course out of our way. Over."

> "U.S. warship, we say again: we cannot move out of your way. Over."

> "Vessel bearing southwest two miles, this is U.S. warship. If you do not move we will ram you. Over."

> "U.S. warship, we are a lighthouse. Your move. Over."

The fine detail of the story may be in doubt, but it highlights the fact that ships' navigators are not always aware that the object that seems to be on collision course with them is a lighthouse. Tidal currents, wind, and fog all help to catch the unwary mariner with some interesting results.

A LAST GOODBYE

In 1913, the American lightship LS 82 was on her normal station off the Lake Erie port of Buffalo, New York, when a sudden storm overwhelmed her and she broke up, killing all her crew. Later, a poignant message was found on a piece of wreckage from the ship. The message was from the lightship master. He had written: "Goodbye Nellie – ship breaking up fast – Williams."

OUT IN THE COLD

Cold weather affects lighthouses in a number of ways. In the days of oil lamps, cold weather would cause the lamp oil to become viscous, which prevented its use. Keepers would then have the risky job of heating it, sometimes with dire results as the oil overheated and caught fire. Many lighthouses across North America suffered from the build-up of ice either on the building during ice storms or with pack ice attempting to push—and some times succeeding in pushing—the towers over. In the winter of 1893 the pile lighthouses in Chesapeake Bay suffered from floating ice. The Wolf Trap Lighthouse was ripped

RIGHT *Assistant Keeper Jan Christiansen taking temperature readings at Oksoy Lighthouse, Kristiansand, Norway. To gain access to the thermometer screen, Jan had to cut a path from the lighthouse through packed snow that was often deeper than he is tall.*

FAR RIGHT *Deep snow surrounds the Ile de Batz Lighthouse on the Brittany coast.*

BOTTOM RIGHT *Ice everywhere you look at St. Joseph's Pier Lighthouse on Lake Michigan. In the era of manned lighthouses on the Great Lakes, the keepers had to chop away the ice by hand using axes, sledge hammers, and crowbars. Even in April and May, to clear the ice from the access doorway often took many days of hard work in appalling conditions.*

from its foundations while the Solomon's Lump Lighthouse suffered the same fate but was found by a passing vessel floating out toward the open sea. It was towed ashore and beached.

Ice build-up is also a major problem in the fresh water of the Great Lakes. The lighthouses are by necessity shut down at the end of the navigation season, the keepers returning before the start of the next season to prepare the lights ready for shipping as soon as the channels thaw. Keepers returning to the Spectacle Reef Lighthouse on Lake Huron in May 1874 found ice piled to a height of ten meters around the lighthouse. They had to hack a way through it to get into the light tower.

During the winter of 1961, an ice storm at the South Head Lighthouse on the coast of Newfoundland trapped two families in their dwellings for nearly 24 hours. The lighthouse is built into a cliff almost 100 feet (30 meters) above the sea. What started as a routine winter's day ended with every building on the station covered by a coat of ice 3 feet (1 meter) thick. Wind carried freezing spray over the station, coating the house to windward, and carrying debris that broke glass in the lantern. The keepers managed to get from the tower to their homes, leaving the lighthouse to fend for itself. Soon, the family in the windward house found that ice had choked their chimney, forcing them to put out their stove. They escaped the now very cold house by crawling across the roof space to the adjoining dwelling, which was in the lee and able to keep its fire alight. When the storm subsided the following afternoon they were able to break out of the house and start clearing up. Help arrived and it took over a week to hack the ice build-up away.

LEFT *Photograph of the charred and blackened Skerryvore Lighthouse, damaged by fire on March 16, 1954. Flames rose to the top of the tower, destroying the lantern.*

ABOVE *Dramatic evidence of the damage to the lantern at Skerryvore Lighthouse following the fire of 1954.*

CONSIGNED TO THE FLAMES

There are many instances of lighthouses burning, not by design as in the previous incident, but through accident. The rays of sunlight falling on the magnifying lens could start fires, though curtains were provided to prevent this and to stop the caulk that held the prisms in place from drying out. Lightning could also cause fires. There have been instances of both causes. Though careful keeping and adherence to operating regulations help, fires do happen. The Hawaiian lighthouse at Makapu'u is one of the major landfall lights in the world. The magnificent hyper-radial lens now has an electric lamp, but in 1925 it was lit by a large oil burner. The alcohol used to prime the kerosene-vapor burner had accidentally dripped on the lantern room floor. One of the keepers, without thinking, lit a match. The explosion that followed killed one of the keepers and badly burned the other. The light was not damaged, but evidence later showed that a fireball had engulfed the room.

A fire at Chicken Rock, a lighthouse off the southern end of the Isle of Man, illustrates how a substantial rock tower can become a roaring chimney fire. On December 23, 1960, the keepers were preparing a meal in the kitchen in the lower part of the lighthouse when fire broke out there. Their escape route was up the tower and out on the gallery to get away from the fire, which was following them up the internal stairway. As the radio telephone in the lighthouse was put out of action by the fire, the keepers set off flares, but to no avail. Finally, using the fog gun, they managed to attract the attention of one of the relief keepers ashore, over three miles away. He realized that there was a problem and promptly alerted the coastguard. Two lifeboats were sent to the scene, but, before the keepers could be taken off, they had to rappel 150 feet (45 meters) from the gallery down to the rocks below. The lifeboat crew rigged a breeches buoy from the rocks to the lifeboat. This was not an easy task, because the weather was poor and the sea rough. The first man down, the assistant keeper, Anderson, made it safely, but suffered severe burns as he came down the rope. He was quickly taken ashore by one of the lifeboats. The two remaining keepers had managed to evacuate the tower, by now blazing out of control, but were unable to get to the waiting lifeboat, because the sea was breaking over the rocks. The tide was rising but their ordeal was not to be over for another four and half hours, until the rescuers managed to snatch the men off the rock during a lull in the breaking seas. The badly damaged lighthouse was repaired and automated—the fire having ended 85 years of manned occupation.

RACE TO THE RESCUE

Not all rescues ended with awards and accolades for the keeper. Thomas Argyle, a former Royal Engineer born in Birmingham, England, found himself the keeper of Race Rock Lighthouse off the shores of British Columbia during the 1870s. In spite of his lack of a nautical background, he was a superb boat handler. Race Rock was named after the fast-flowing tides that surrounded it, but he had no thought of danger as he launched his boat to rescue two men he had spotted drifting by on logs. Later, in court on the mainland, he may have regretted his brave action: he was fined $100 (two months' pay) for "aiding and abetting two seaman deserters from H.M.S. *Shah* to escape"!

KEEPER AS LIFESAVER

In 1870 the iron tower of Point Reyes Lighthouse was built in a niche 295 feet (90 meters) above the Pacific Ocean on the Californian coast north of San Francisco.

From their high vantage point the keepers could watch the busy coastal shipping lane and the fishing vessels working below. The keeper, Fred Kreth, was doing just that when he noticed that a fishing boat had struck the rocks right below him. He watched with concern as the three crewmen struggled to a narrow ledge ashore to await rescue by the coastguard. The keeper—assessing the situation of rising tide and rough sea—knew that the rescue boat would not be able to get the men off, so he pulled a rope from his store and prepared to go down the cliff face. The wind sent him crashing against the rocks, bruising and cutting him. While he was on his way down, the rescue boat arrived and signaled to the waiting men that they would be rescued from the cliff top. The crew of the boat had not noticed Keeper Kreth on his way down, so sailed away to organize a coastguard rescue crew.

Hours later, the cliff team arrived and descended to get the men, but could not find them. They assumed that they had been swept away or had attempted to swim to safety. The team went to the lighthouse to raise the alarm and initiate a coastal search. They found the keeper and the fishermen safe in the lighthouse, recovering from the ordeal. Fred Kreth received a commendation for his lone act of bravery.

BELOW *The long steps down the cliff to Point Reyes Lighthouse on the California coast.*

Chapter 6 | LIGHTSHIPS AND RELIEF VESSELS

In 1728 two London merchants, Robert Hamblin and Nicholas Avery, thought that providing a light on the Nore Sands in the Thames Estuary of the U.K. would be a good idea. It was, and it was to become the first ever lightship.

The light, they reasoned, would help to prevent ships inward-bound for London from straying into the extensive shoal water, grounding and losing valuable cargo. The project was also a potential moneymaker, because fellow merchants and ship owners could be charged dues every time their ships docked at the wharves of London. They could not build a lighthouse on the shifting sands, so they decided to anchor a floating lighthouse or lightship on the seaward edge of the sand.

THE IDEA SEEMED CRAZY, FOR THEIR lightship would have to withstand storms that would send prudent seamen running for shelter. They would have to find men willing to live an uncomfortable life on board what would be no better than a rolling, pitching, wet prison cell. Those chosen would have to be trustworthy and skillful enough to keep the light burning even in bad weather. There was also great opposition from Trinity House, who thought that the

The terms "lightship" and "light vessel" are interchangeable. Americans prefer the former; Europeans the latter. This is why the term LV is used before the number of a lightship. For example, Trinity House Light Vessel LV22 is on the Varne station off southern England (the actual ship is designated ALV22, because she is automatic). In the U.S., both LV and LS are used. After the Coastguards took over they were designated WAL.

proposed lightship would always be breaking adrift and would be a danger rather than a help to navigation. However, political pressure and lobbying by London merchants enabled Hamblin and Avery's petition to the Crown to succeed, but not until some years later: 1730, in fact, when they were eventually granted a patent.

This first lightship was converted from a trading sloop about 40 feet (12 meters) long and displacing about 50 tons. It was hardly the ideal vessel, with bluff bows and a flat bottom, a hull shape that would have caused it to bob about like a cork in the short steep waters of the estuary. Hardly the ideal platform for the light or comfortable for the keepers. The light comprised two candle lanterns hung

RIGHT *The Abertay light vessel in dock for maintenance. Note the high bow and the solid construction necessary to withstand the onslaught of the sea.*

from the ends of the yardarm so that they could be lowered to the deck for lighting or replacement. The hapless crew were accommodated in a makeshift shelter on the deck, while the stores were carried in the hold. During storms there was no shelter to protect the men so they could tend the light—indeed, the decks would have been awash as the waves swept over the vessel, and lighting the light would be like trying to light a cigarette in a shower. The anchors and warps were primitive and not really strong enough for the job. The lightship broke from its moorings on numerous occasions, just as Trinity House had said it would! When this happened the vessel's supporting tender had to find and tow it back to its correct station. Nevertheless, the idea worked, and shipmasters using it considered it a great help. They asked for more lightships to be positioned on the sandbanks of the east coast and on the Goodwin Sands off southeast Kent.

Though the Nore vessel is considered to be the first lightship, the Dutch had suggested in a Dutch–Danish treaty of 1669 the use of a "floating light" to guide ships past the island of Anholt in the stormy strait of Kattegat. The idea was not taken up, though many years later, in 1842, a lightship was placed to the east of the island, but was replaced by a lighthouse in 1852.

The Romans, too, had a form of lightship: their coastguard ships—known as *liburnae*—patrolled the entrances to harbors. When a friendly ship was sighted, a fire basket at the top of the mast was lit, and the ship was guided safely into port. It is not difficult to imagine that similar tactics could have been used to guide enemy ships into dangerous water in order to wreck them.

In 1807, Robert Stevenson used a lightship called the *Pharos* to mark the site of his proposed Bell Rock lighthouse. The lightship, because it marked the

rock, could start charging light dues—but, more importantly, it provided a floating base for Stevenson and his workforce. This temporary use of lightships was by no means a rarity. Sir James Douglass, engineer-in-chief to Trinity House from 1863 to 1892, used lightships at the Basses reefs off the east of Sri Lanka in 1863 and at Eddystone off Plymouth, U.K., in 1880 during the building of the fourth lighthouse there. They were used in the last century at Skerryvore, Scotland, after a fire in 1954 gutted it and put it out of action while repairs were carried out, and at Bull Point lighthouse, North Devon, to provide a temporary light after the lighthouse on the cliffs fell into the sea in 1975.

On the surface, the idea of a lightship seems a good one, but it was not quite as simple an answer as it first seemed. The major problem that the pioneer lightship owners faced was finding a way of keeping the light exhibited on the chosen station even in the worst weather. If the light was not in place when needed, complaints soon flowed in from the shipmasters who paid for it and relied on it to be where they expected it to be! The other problem was to keep the light burning when rain, wind, and spray were trying to douse it, while the constantly rolling and pitching lightship did its utmost to thwart the men tending the light.

Methods of anchoring ships were not a precise science: an iron or stone sinker weight attached to a poor-quality rope was the only way a ship could be anchored. To tend the ship and its light, tough men were needed, with iron constitutions. Imagine living and working in a leaking, swaying prison—for that was just what was

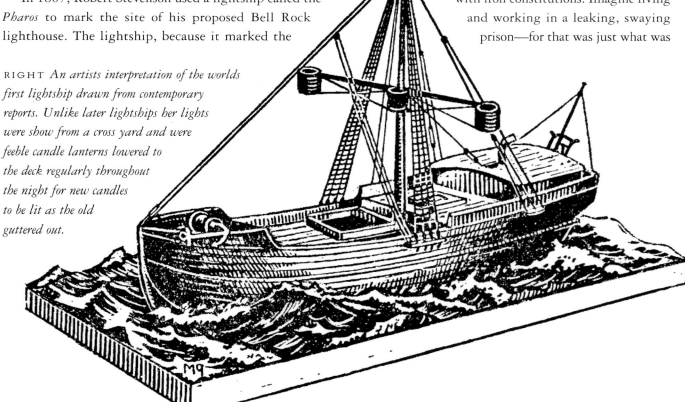

RIGHT *An artists interpretation of the worlds first lightship drawn from contemporary reports. Unlike later lightships her lights were show from a cross yard and were feeble candle lanterns lowered to the deck regularly throughout the night for new candles to be lit as the old guttered out.*

NORE

ABOVE *The Nore light vessel at St Catherine's Dock, London, England.*

expected of the lightship keepers. Even compared with seagoing in those early days it was a rugged way of life. The attraction, if it could be called that, to the seaman was that it was regular work and regular pay, while, for the married man, it gave a reasonable chance of being home on a regular basis rather than wandering the world.

And so, while in some ways it seemed that there was less going for the idea of lightships than for it, Trinity House eventually adopted the concept. In spite of their early resistance and misgivings, they now agreed with ship owners and masters that they were useful aids to the navigator and contributed to safety at sea. By 1832, they had stationed their first five ships, all on the east coast sandbanks to complement the coastal lights of Yorkshire and East Anglia. These lights were on the trade route used by the hundreds of collier ships carrying coal between the northeast coast ports and London. Lightships, though cheap to place on station, were much more expensive to maintain than a lighthouse. There was more wear and tear, for instance, the need for large crews, and the fact that the lightship needed to have a second ship and crew standing by to be ready to take her back to station when she broke adrift.

The early lightships had the same type of simple hanging lantern as the Nore lightship. But in 1807, Robert Stevenson invented a lantern house that could be raised and lowered by the crew so that the oil lamps could be maintained. This design also improved the light output, as a number of Argand lamps and reflectors could now be fitted to increase the amount of light. This design was to remain in service until replaced by the fixed lantern developed by Trinity House in the 1930s. German and American lightships, however, chose to use high-intensity beacons on the top of conventional masts.

The use of lightships grew rapidly throughout the world. During the next century they were used to mark shallow waters and sandbanks off the coasts of Ireland, Denmark, Germany, and Sweden. British colonial administrators used them to assist the trading and naval ships using the newly founded ports from tropical Calcutta to the channels of the Canadian St. Lawrence River.

SLOW TO SEE THE LIGHT

The United States was slow to use lightships, mainly because of the resistance by Stephen Pleasanton, the Fifth Auditor, who thought that they did not give value for money and was concerned about the high cost of keeping them on station. In 1820 he relented and authorized, as an experiment, the placing of a lightship on the

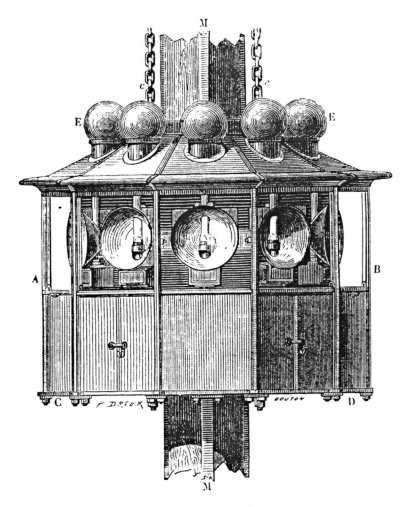

ABOVE AND LEFT *A lightship lantern house designed by Robert Stevenson. It could be lowered for lamp cleaning and lighting, and then raised by chain to its working position at the top of the substantial mast. The lantern house encircled the mast to give a light that was visible all around.*

Willoughby shoal in the shallow waters off the Virginia coast. The site was, however, too rough for the small 70-ton vessel, so she was moved to Craney Island, near Norfolk. The experiment must have been successful, for the following year four more were authorized for Chesapeake Bay. These first five U.S. lightships were all in embayments and relatively calm waters. The first to be put on a station open to the Atlantic Ocean was placed six miles off the New Jersey shore at Sandy Hook in 1823. It was placed there to augment the lighthouses at Sandy Hook and Navesink, assisting ships making for New York. This station remained in use until it was replaced by the Ambrose Channel lightship, owing to changes in the New York approaches.

The ships engaged in the growing coastal trade between New York and the southern states all had to negotiate the vast area of sandbanks off the Carolina coastline. Many did not survive the sudden storms of the area, or else they piled onto the unmarked banks. A number of lighthouses were built on the distant low-lying shore, but Congress had made its intentions clear in 1806, when it demanded that a scheme for an offshore lighthouse be examined. When Congressmen were told that it was not feasible, the idea was dropped until the 1820s, when it was decided that a lightship should be placed in the deep water outside off Cape Hatteras—Diamond Shoals, as it was also known.

Courage was needed, not only by those making the decision to place a light so far offshore—it was almost 14 miles off the coast, about 3 hours' sailing time from the nearest port—but also by those brave enough to crew the lightship. The Hatteras—or Diamond Shoals—lightship was anchored in 180 feet (55 meters) of water in 1824 and managed to stay on station for almost a year. In 1825 the lightship broke from its mooring during a gale. Luckily, the vessel had rudimentary sails, so was able to make for Norfolk, where it stayed for almost a year. Just before Christmas it was put back on station but stayed put for only five months before the same thing happened again. The ship and crew stayed in port until November, when they set out again for the station, this time managing to remain there until a gale in August 1827 finally drove the unlucky lightship ashore. One account says that she was

TOP RIGHT *An 1891 illstration of the Nantucket New South Shoal Lightship, showing the typical sea conditions endured by lightship crews on the Atlantic coast. The Nantucket New South Shoal Lightship was stationed offshore in open waters. Note the oil lamps on each mast.*

LEFT *Irish light vessel, Kishbank, off the Dublin coast.*

returned to the sea after a channel was dredged to enable her to be floated off; another that she was broken up for salvage where she lay.

Lightships were not used on the Diamond Shoals for another 70 years. The conditions had beaten all who tried. Though a vessel was eventually placed on the shoal, it is fairly certain from the events outlined that no one was serious about lightships. If they had been, such a vessel would not have been allowed remain off station for so long. The hope was that a permanent lighthouse could be built. Nothing was done about the problem until the 1870s, when various lighthouse schemes were put forward. An attempt was made to build a lighthouse on the edge of the shoal in the early 1880s, but it came to nothing because storms destroyed the first stages of the construction, and the Lighthouse Board were then prevailed upon to provide a lightship.

By 1897 lightship design and anchoring methods had improved and so a new vessel was placed on the Diamond Shoals station. The first had used an anchor of about 1,200 pounds (540 kilograms) and a natural-fiber rope, which was totally inadequate, but the new lightship had a cast-iron anchor weighing 5,000 pounds (2,270 kilograms) and a 3-inch (75-millimeter) chain—each link was 12 inches

long (60 centimeters) and weighed 20 lbs—which was able to hold the ship even in the most severe conditions. The lightships now stationed on the Diamond Shoals stayed where they were needed, until replaced by a Texas Tower in 1966. Indeed, the last ship on the station, in the 1960s, had an anchor and ground chain weighing a total of 31,000 pounds/14,000 kilograms. (Texas Towers were built as oil rigs, but are now used all over the world as light towers.)

There were many instances of the lightships on the American ocean stations being driven ashore or being abandoned by their crews after breaking adrift. Some lucky crews were rescued; others were lost without trace. The crew of the Columbia Lightship were among the lucky ones! The ship also survived and returned to station, but only after a railway journey. The story started on a November night in 1899. A hurricane with 75-mile-an-hour winds off the Pacific coast of Oregon blasted the lightship, rolling her, washing her decks with tons of green water and eventually breaking the 2-inch-diameter (50-millimeter) links of her anchor chain. As she was sail-powered, her captain, whose name is unknown, made the decision to stay well offshore and ride out the wind and the high seas. The sturdy ship weathered the storm until the next day, when the captain judged he could make harbor safely.

He set course for the Columbia River, where he was met by tugs to assist him over the pounding seas of the entrance bar and into safety. But all did not to go to plan.

ABOVE *Trinity House's Channel light vessel under tow during a heavy storm. The two chain cables connect to the towing vessel from where the photograph was taken.*

OPPOSITE TOP *Columbia lightship, LS 50, on her way back to the sea by rail after being stranded.*

OPPOSITE BOTTOM *WAL 605—the U.S. lightship rescued and restored by the United States Lighthouse Society. She is berthed in Oakland, California. This painting by Ralph B. Starr was sold to raise funds for the vessel's restoration.*

One of the tugs fouled its own propeller with a hawser, and the other managed to get a towline aboard the lightship, only to have it part at a critical point just inside the entrance. The lightship captain saw that his ship was not going to get over the bar safely and, rather than risk her crashing on the rocks, he deliberately beached her with her bows pointing out to sea and her stern well up a beach.

The crew escaped by breeches buoy to the shore with their ship left high and dry. Subsequent attempts to refloat her failed. After much deliberation, it was decided that the only way was overland to a bay about half a mile (1 kilometer) distant. Contractors were engaged to do the job. First they dug out all the sand that had accumulated in the hull, and then they turned the ship around to face inland. At the time this was going on a railway track was

TOP LEFT *The Seven Stones light vessel protects shipping from the reef of the same name to the north of the Isles of Scilly. This lightship is moored in deeper water than is usual and, although in an exposed position, was a popular posting because the deeper water meant a less turbulent ride.*

BOTTOM LEFT *Ballycotton lifeboat rescues the crew of the Irish lightship Comet. The lightship was on the Daunt station off the southeast coast of Ireland when she parted from her moorings during a violent storm on February 10, 1936. The crew saved the lightship by dropping the reserve anchor and were taken off only after they had become exhausted after days and nights without rest or sleep.*

ABOVE *A modern automatic unmanned lightvessel.*

laid through woodland to the next bay. The lightship was jacked onto a carrying bogie and slowly hauled onto the railway back to the sea. She was repaired at a cost of $14,000 and returned to her station in May 1902.

DISASTERS IN EUROPE
Disasters to lightships were not confined to United States waters. Many European light vessels recorded ships running them down, usually striking a glancing blow and sliding away into the mist. The East Goodwin lightship, one of the group protecting ships from the notorious sands of the Dover Straits between England and France, was run down in 1902 by a large steamer heading down channel.

The accident was to make maritime radio history, for it was the first time radio was used to summon rescue at sea. The collision happened during the experiments that the radio pioneer Marconi was carrying out for Trinity House at the North Foreland Lighthouse, Kent, England. He was investigating the possibility of using radio to communicate between ship and shore, so had fitted a radio to the lightship some days before the incident. The lightship master was able to send a message ashore to the North Foreland Lighthouse operator, who alerted the coastguards to the lightship's predicament. The Dover lifeboat was launched and the lightship crew rescued. The lightship was repaired and replaced on its station. The resulting publicity, which made people aware of the value of radio communication, was said to have helped Marconi to raise capital to continue his experiments.

In 1912, the Belgian West Hinder lightship was not even on her station when she was fatally damaged. While under tow on her way into harbor with her crew on board she was in collision with a string of pontoon barges, as a result of which she was rolled over and so badly damaged that she sank immediately, drowning her crew of ten.

World War I started as a "gentlemen's" war as far as aids to navigation were concerned, with lighthouses and lightships respected by both sides. The crews of the lightships kept their lights exhibited more or less as they had in peacetime, with the added task of rescuing and sustaining crews of ships sunk by enemy action. Sometimes overzealous airmen would use the lanterns for target practice, but the crews were respected. Toward the end of the war, the threat of submarine activity increased. The Commissioners of Irish Lights lost one of their lightships to enemy action on the night of March 28, 1917, when a German submarine sank the lightship on the Arklow station off the east coast of Ireland. After the war the new German government paid £17,000 as reparations to build a replacement vessel.

The lightship on the Diamond Shoals, North Carolina, suffered the same fate on August 6, 1918. The vessel's radio operator had been warning shipping that a German submarine was in the area, but, unfortunately for the lightship crew, the operator on the U-boat intercepted his calls. So the submarine surfaced, ordered the lightship crew into boats, and then sank the lightship to punish the crew for giving away its position!

MANY HANDS MAKE LIGHTS WORK

By 1930, more than 500 lightships were stationed world-wide, employing thousands of crew. Some lightships had additional duties as weather stations, radio stations, and pilot stations. The decade was also one of technical improvement, with all-electric ships taking over from the oil lamp, both for the main light and for the lighting and operation of the ship's equipment. The crew comfort had increased, too, with vessels heated by coal- or oil-fired central heating. Radios were available not only for ship-to-shore communication, but also for crews to be able to listen to broadcast programs in their leisure time. The life

on a lightship, as we saw earlier, was at best equated to being in a floating, wet prison, though the more modern ships with better facilities helped. However, life aboard a lightship was still, for some people, a boring existence. Some crewmen could stand only one tour of duty, but for many it was an enjoyable way of life.

Many lightsmen were capable model makers and skilled in a wide range of handicrafts. Sweaters were knitted and tapestries made, but the traditional craft was rope work. This is said to date from the time when a lightship inspector was concerned that the crews of vessels within his jurisdiction might become bored and mutinous. He placed rope on board the lightships with instructions that rope mats and rope-soled canvas shoes could be made by the men, and sold when they went ashore on leave. He reasoned that the work would prevent idle mischief and that the extra money would be popular. Fishing for sport and food was a popular pastime for many crewmen, too, with some record catches recorded.

BELOW *Christmas on a lightship was one occasion when the dreary monotony of the daily chores could be replaced for an hour or so by a festive meal and a game of cards. Christmas cards cheered the lightships and many lightships received Christmas visitors.*

RIGHT *This Trinity House light vessel, LV 91, was built at Dartmouth, England, in 1937 and served until 1980, then became a floating museum in Swansea, South Wales.*

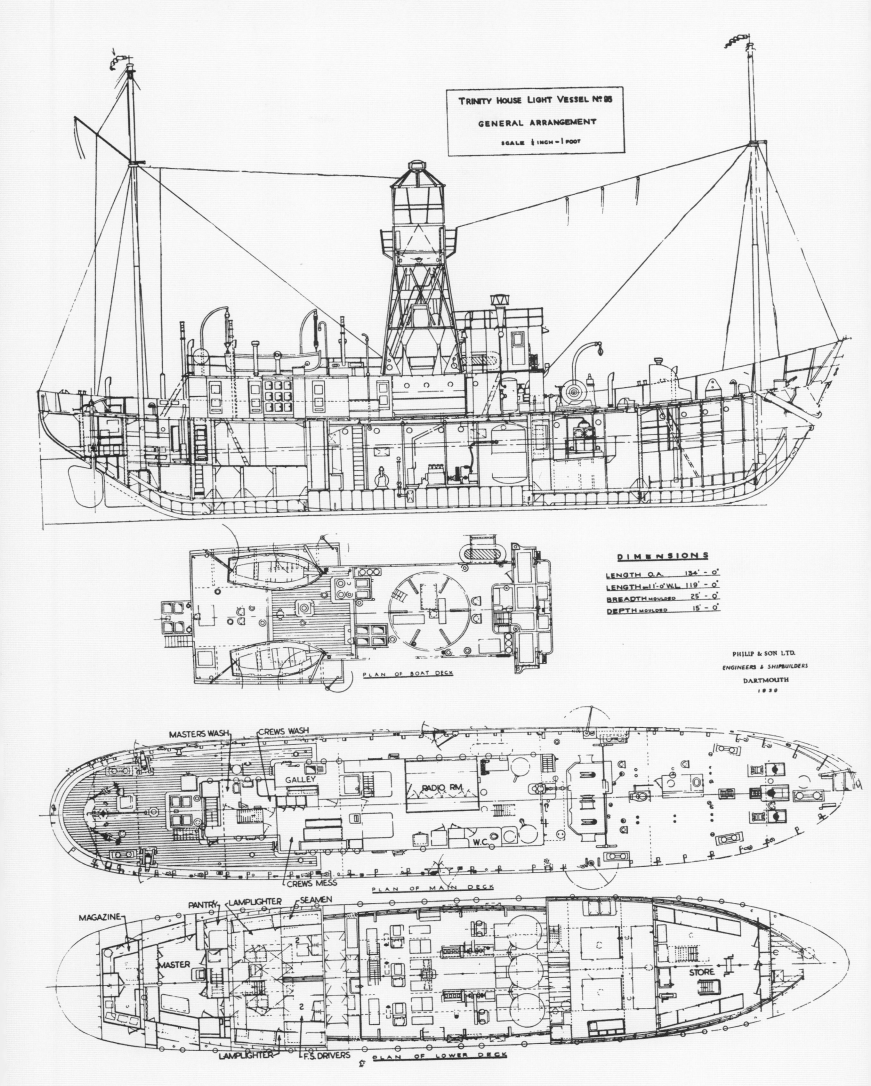

TRINITY HOUSE LIGHT VESSEL Nᵒ 95

GENERAL ARRANGEMENT

SCALE ¼ INCH = 1 FOOT

DIMENSIONS

LENGTH O.A.   134' - 0"
LENGTH on 1'-0" W.L   119' - 0"
BREADTH MOULDED   25' - 0"
DEPTH MOULDED   15' - 0"

PHILIP & SON LTD.
ENGINEERS & SHIPBUILDERS
DARTMOUTH
1939

PLAN OF BOAT DECK

MASTERS WASH   CREWS WASH
GALLEY
RADIO RM.
W.C.
CREWS MESS
PLAN OF MAIN DECK

MAGAZINE
PANTRY   LAMPLIGHTER   SEAMEN
MASTER
STORE
LAMPLIGHTER   F.S. DRIVERS   PLAN OF LOWER DECK

No. 93 Light Vessel

THE NANTUCKET DISASTER

The 11-man crew of LS No. 117, stationed on the Nantucket shoal on May 13, 1934, settled down after breakfast to carry out their daily routines. As was quite usual on the station, thick fog developed and the fog signal, a bellowing diaphone horn, was switched on. The crew thought that all ships in the vicinity would hear their warning signal and steer away from them and the shoal waters that they were guarding. What they did not know was that, by a quirk of the weather, their warning had not been picked up by the approaching White Star liner *Olympic*. The 47,000-ton leviathan was rapidly approaching them. Suddenly out of the fog the *Olympic*'s bow appeared too late for the lightship to move or give warning of her presence.

The liner cut the lightship in half. One half sank immediately, while the other remained afloat long enough for some of the crew to be saved. The liner stopped, lowered lifeboats, and managed to rescue seven of the crew—four had died during the collision—but three of those saved were to succumb later.

The White Star line replaced the lightship and paid compensation to the survivors and the families of the dead men.

BELOW *The fatal moment. An artist's impression of the last minutes of LS 117 as the Olympic's razor-sharp bow cuts her in two.*

Life on board lightships by the 1930s had improved. The design of the ships, with more sea worthy hulls, the addition of stabilizing bilge keels, and an improvement in the quality of the accommodation, made life more tolerable. Some ships carried cooks, and on Danish ships there were even stewardesses to look after the catering arrangements. For the men on the Trinity House lightships, the cooking routine was unique. Each man had his own stores, which he purchased and took on board. These were kept separate and each man prepared his own meal, using meat, potatoes, and vegetables of his choice, which he put in a net bag. This was cooked on a coal-fired cooking range by one of the crew. The duty cook would put a large pan of water onto the range, into which he would place each man's net of food to heat up. In America, lightships were assigned cooks.

TOO CLOSE FOR COMFORT

The crews of lightships stationed in busy shipping lanes and in the entrances to harbors were aware that they were sitting targets for badly navigated ships. In the days of sail, the worst that could happen was that a sailing ship would drift into the lightship, causing only minor damage. The advent of steam- and motor-driven ships changed that. There were many times when an approaching ship would spot the anchored lightship and veer away just in the last few heart-stopping moments before disaster. There were other times when the fears of the seamen on the lightships were totally justified.

Compared with World War I, when lightships were usually left alone without interference, World War II was total war, with neither side allowing aids to navigation to

ABOVE *The Nantucket light vessel.*

continue in operation unmolested. As the Nazis overran Europe, the lightships of the European coast from Holland to the Atlantic were captured and in many cases taken back to Germany or converted to other uses. Danish lightships were moved from offshore waters to the relative safety of the inshore sounds. The lightships of Britain and Ireland remained on their stations at the start of the war. This was to change as lightships became targets for enemy aircraft and ships. With their radios, the lightships were able to report enemy movements and were therefore classed as belligerent vessels. The lightship at Smith's Knoll in the North Sea was attacked on January 11, 1940, this being the first of more than 100 reported attacks. Many lightships were sunk at their moorings, though most did not have permanent crews. The final total was 20 lightships lost to enemy action.

During the hostilities, the lightship station names were painted over and the lights extinguished, but for the first years of the war the crews remained on board. They were at risk from raiders both by sea and air, with the menace of floating mines an added concern. To combat this risk, a sharp lookout was kept and a crewman with a rifle stood by to hopefully detonate any mine spotted a safe distance from the ship. A successful shot saved the lightship, with the bonus of stunned fish that could be collected by launching the lifeboat to gather them in.

George Carter, who served on English lightships during the early period of the war, recorded how they would watch as passing ships were blown out of the water, leaving them surrounded by the debris of war. Sometimes they salvaged cargo. He remembered once getting a case of bananas.

The crew of the East Dudgeon lightship off the north Norfolk coast of England were not so fortunate. Around mid-1940, they were attacked by enemy planes, and took to their lifeboat to escape the bombs and bullets. When the raiders had flown off they returned unharmed to their damaged—but still afloat—lightship. Perhaps they were spotted, maybe it was different aircraft, but there came a second attack! Once more, they boarded their lifeboat. By now, the wind and sea had risen and they made a decision to row for the shore 20 miles away. Throughout the night they rowed hard until, at dawn, they saw the coast. Sadly, when almost safe, the lifeboat was turned over by breaking seas and the men were all thrown out. Nevertheless, they made the shore. Injury and exhaustion took their toll and all but one man died of exposure on the beach before they could be rescued.

After that incident the lightships were demanned and a small crew placed on board only when the light was needed for a friendly passing coastal convoy. Some were removed from their peacetime stations and placed at strategic points called "war stations." The North Carr Lightship, one of only a few Scottish lightships, was moved from her normal home off the north shore of the Firth of Forth on the east coast in 1943 to a station in the entrance to the Clyde. She was used as a homing mark for the inward-bound troop convoys from the U.S.A. Others were placed at the boomed entrances to ports to mark them, and they were supported by armed boom-defense vessels. Twenty English lightships were lost and 27 lightsmen lost their lives due to enemy action.

Two lightships gained fame when they were manned up and towed in the wake of the D-Day forces to mark channels through the minefields off Normandy in June 1944. The Kansas Lightship marked the channel into Cherbourg and the *Juno* the channel into the temporary Mulberry harbor. LV *Juno* was built by John Crown of Sunderland in 1903 as "LV72" for Trinity House, and served on east coast stations until she was removed from station in 1940 and taken into Yarmouth. When needed for Normandy, she was taken to Cowes on the Isle of Wight to be prepared and equipped with stores and towed to her war station on June 17, 1994. As the Allied forces gained ground in France, she was moved to mark the entrance to Le Havre and the River Seine before returning to Harwich in Essex for refit and modernization. Then she returned on 3 April, 1946, to her peacetime station at Smith's Knoll. In 1953 she was moved to work on the Welsh stations, from where she was retired in 1973. She now lies derelict in a South Wales river.

BELOW *Relief at the Breaksea lightship off South Wales, U.K. The tender lies off and the launch plies to and fro with stores and men — a hazardous job unless the sea was flat-calm.*

Many lightships were replaced by buoys or lighthouses after the war. Some were used off the European coasts to make safe channels through uncleared minefields, though this role was a temporary one, as all lightships on this duty were withdrawn by the mid-1950s. In North America, unmanned LANBYs (Large Automatic Navigation Buoys) and tubular-steel Texas Towers replaced many lightships, so that by 1970 there were very few left in service. Trinity House, however, made the decision to replace their war losses with new all-steel ships. The 21 ships were built at the Phillips shipyard between 1946 and 1956. All were designed as manned ships but since the 1980s have all been converted to automatic operation. Some, not required, have been sold out of service for new lives as floating museums or even as public bars.

LIGHT RELIEF . . .

The crews of lightships and the offshore lighthouses, at whatever stage of their history, had one common thought when on duty: would the relief tender be on time? A late relief means a shortage of food and a reduced leave period. The harsh rule was that leave started from the *official* day of relief rather than the actual day that it happened, so it was too bad if it was a week or fortnight late because of bad weather conditions. For the oncoming crew it was no better: they had left home prepared to go on duty, only to find that they either spent hours waiting on a windswept quay or, worse, left bouncing around for days on the relief tender.

So relief day arrived. The men being transferred from lightship or lighthouse faced a hazardous trip in a small boat, almost always wet and cold whatever time of year. For the men staying on duty was the knowledge that they had another month to spend there, though mail, fresh newspapers, and stores no doubt relieved the prospect.

Aboard the lightship, as soon as contact had been made with the approaching relief tender, the scene would be one of frantic activity. Bedding, a personal kit, and equipment packed to go ashore for repair would be placed on deck ready to be placed in the tender's boat. The boat would arrive, sometimes, if the sea was rough, high above the waiting men, dropping into a trough in the waves. With water and spray everywhere, the relieving men would grasp their opportunity and leap aboard the lightship, followed quickly by all their stores. The men going off would then board the boat, followed by all the boxes and baggage—in the U.S. the men took very little ashore unless they were being transferred. Once they were safely

ABOVE *Relief on an unusually calm day at Hanois Lighthouse, Guernsey, Channel Islands.*

LEFT *Many keepers got a soaking while being transferred from launch to lighthouse steps by rope. This relief is being carried out at the Bishop Rock lighthouse, Isles of Scilly, in the days of boat relief. The now unmanned lighthouse has a helipad for occasional visits by technicians.*

BELOW LEFT *Relief tender arriving at the Rotersand Lighthouse at the mouth of the River Elbe. This photograph was talken in 1928, but the occasional visits from technicians now are still carried out in the same way.*

stowed, the boat made its way to the tender lying some distance, away where the process was repeated. This was not for either the faint hearted or poor seaman. To complete a relief the boat would make as many trips as needed, each one requiring skill and judgment gained only after years of experience. Sometimes, unusual loads were moved, particularly to lighthouses. When the lighthouse keepers on the Scottish island of Islay needed a new tractor, it was delivered from the tender on a platform made by lashing timbers across two boats.

The tenders carrying out the relief were sturdy, small ships; in the early days they were sailing ships manned by some of the most expert seamen of their day. They, like their modern counterparts, navigated their crafts in places that the seaman would normally avoid. They were experts at pilotage in rocky coastal waters, often in poor weather conditions. When sail was replaced first by steam vessels and later by diesel-engined ships, the expertise remained.

Considering the amount of time that tenders have spent in dangerous waters, recorded accidents are very few. In 1992, for example, the Irish lighthouse tender *Granuiaille* had the misfortune to strike a submerged rock off the Northern Ireland coast. At the time she was working in the swirling waters off the Maidens Rocks, taking the Commissioners of Irish Lights on their annual inspection to the Maidens Lighthouse. She foundered on the jagged rocks and started to take in water. Though starting to sink, she managed to make her way toward the nearest harbor, which was about eight miles away at Larne, Country Antrim. The ingress of water was too much for the ship's pumps, however, and the engine was put out of action. All but essential crewmen took to the lifeboats, while two tugs that had arrived on the scene took the sinking ship in tow. They towed her into shallow water, where she was beached and later salvaged. After refit she returned to service. In a subsequent report, an unnamed journalist wrote:

It always seems so much worse when a vessel charged with the maintenance of navigational aids, almost by definition manned by navigation perfectionists runs aground … Bearing in mind the way in which lighthouse tenders spend all their days a few cables [a cable is about a tenth of a nautical mile] off rocky coasts that other mariners steer clear of, it's a wonder it does not happen more often.

The use of helicopters in the U.K. transformed the task of relieving the remaining manned lighthouses and lightships, and, because of the relative ease with which men could be put on board, helped to hasten the demanning process. Lightships and lighthouses were fitted with helicopter landing pads. On a lightship the aftermost mast was removed and an additional deck was built; on a lighthouse site, if no clear area was available, the lantern dome was removed and the pad assembled on the top. On relief day the crew going onto the lightship board the helicopter with all their stores and fly out to the rolling, swaying heli-deck of the lightship. On arrival, the pilot, judging his time, landed on the deck, keeping the rotors turning to hold the helicopter in place while the men and their stores were quickly unloaded. The relief took just a few minutes, compared with the hours of struggle when this operation had to be done by boat. Heavy loads such as

ABOVE Bishop Rock lighthouse off the Isles of Scilly in the southwestern approaches to the U.K. This is relief the easy way: the helicopter can land on the specially constructed landing pad in almost any weather except thick fog. A hatch allows access into the lantern room and the living quarters below.

fresh water or fuel oil in 100-gallon (380-liter) rubber bags or spare parts in cargo nets are carried underneath the aircraft and delivered without the need for landing.

The helicopter was just one of the advances in technology that changed the way that offshore lighthouses and lightships were operated. The universal use of electricity or gas decreased the daily workload of the men keeping the lights. The ease of access meant that lighthouses and light vessels could be maintained by crews flown out to them, and the light and fog signal monitored remotely by a radio telemetry system. By the use of backup systems, faults could be corrected automatically.

Many countries, including the United States, withdrew their lightships from service, replacing them with fixed structures or automatic buoys. Some countries, England among them, kept lightships, but made them totally automatic in operation, and by the end of the twentieth century were using solar power to provide the electricity for operation. The days of men suffering in rolling storm-ridden prisons were over.

LEFT *The Inner Dowsing Light Tower off England's East Coast was converted from an undersea coal exploration rig.*

LEFT (INSET) *An American Light Tower based on a Texas Tower as developed by the offshore Oil Industry.*

RIGHT *Canadian Coastguard buoy tender, Sir Wilfrid Laurier, making its way through ice.*

RIGHT *Trinity House tender, Patricia, lifting the Elbow Buoy in the Thames Estuary from her foredeck, after maintenance has been carried out, to replace it on its station.*

BELOW *The U.S. Coast Guard tender, Juniper (WALB-201), during her sea trials before taking up service on the Great Lakes in 1996.*

Chapter 7 | THE AGE OF RESPLENDENCE

Some early lighthouses were poorly built—merely mounds of stone, just enough to hold the beacon fire in place. Others, as we saw in earlier chapters (such as the Pharos at Alexandria and the Roman lighthouses at Ostia, Dover, and other parts of the Roman Empire), may have had architectural merit, though they have not survived for modern judgment. There are no longer many examples of the medieval structures left— those that have survived are a tribute to their builders. However, the lighthouses from the 19th century, the heyday of lighthouse building, have survived and are in many cases still in operation. This chapter will explore the varied designs, materials used and methods of construction that were used in this golden age.

THE DESIGN OF THE LIGHTHOUSE buildings has always been influenced by a number of factors. The location and accessibility of the proposed site, for instance, were of prime importance. In some parts of the world—North America, Australia, and other locations—major exploration was necessary before the planned location of a lighthouse in inaccessible areas could even be confirmed. Cape Otway lighthouse on the Bass Strait shore, Australia, (see Chapter 4) is a good example of the effort needed before any work was even attempted on the site. The Colonial Architect, Mortimer Lewis, who designed that lighthouse, needed to know that the site was suitable and that he could get his materials and labor there. The superintendent of the Port Philip district of New South Wales, Charles La Trobe, who was responsible for organizing this, did not let Lewis down.

La Trobe produced a detailed surveyors' report in 1846 that was instrumental to the success of the contract, though he did omit to calculate the huge amount of sand

above bedrock. This was an omission that was to cause some problems once the work started, leading to the actual tower's having to be built some 50 feet (15 meters) away from the original surveyed site!

Charles Tyers, a Crown Lands Commissioner who at the same time had been sent to look at the site at Gabo Island at the eastern end of the Bass Strait, was not as diligent. As soon as the lighthouse design was completed the following year, Mortimer Lewis placed the building contract. The contractors moved onto the island and started to dig the foundations, but were unable or did not have the expertise to build on the site. A naval officer, Captain Owen Stanley, visiting the island to inspect the works in March 1848, noted that all there was to show for all the construction efforts was a hole in the sand 60 feet

RIGHT *The chalk cliffs tower above Beachy Head Lighthouse. A cliff fall in 2000 linked the lighthouse to the land by filling the gap and providing a chalk bridge.*

(18 meters) deep. What Charles Tyers had missed was that firm bedrock could not be found near the surface. The contractor was dismissed and the workings abandoned.

The available surveyors' and builders' expertise was to be the bane of many early designers. Stephen Pleasonton, the Fifth Auditor of the U.S. Treasury, was a constant critic of the skills of the contractors employed to build American lighthouses during his tenure of office, which lasted from 1820 to 1852. Designers also had to balance the requirements of the mariners for the best possible light against the parsimony of the funding authority, which invariably wanted the cheapest building rather than the best.

Money, however, had not always been the problem. Nearly 300 years before, Louis de Foix, the French architect who had been responsible for the public buildings in Bayonne, a city in the southwest of France, was contracted to build a lighthouse regardless of expense. In 1584, he started to build his structure at Cordouan in the entrance to the Gironde estuary on the West Coast of France.

THE STORY OF A LIGHTHOUSE

The story of Corduoan lighthouse exemplifies the progression of design throughout lighthouse history. The estuary that it still marks today is open to the prevailing westerly winds from the Atlantic. But, back in the days of sail, vessels would be driven into the entrance by bad weather, trapped and wrecked on one of the many sandbanks. Most of the wrecked ships were engaged in the Gascony wine trade from the port of Bordeaux further up the estuary. In the ninth century, the citizens of that town petitioned Louis the

RIGHT *The ornate decoration of Cordouan lighthouse had no functional purpose. The architect, Louis de Foix, designed it to please his king.*

Pious (814–40), son of Charlemagne, for permission to erect a beacon fire on a small spit of land in the entrance to the waterway. No record remains of the design or construction of this first light. It must have been a fairly substantial structure, though, since it remained in place, if not in use, until removed by workmen employed by Edward the Black Prince (1330–76).

A document dated 1409 tells us about the replacement lighthouse erected under Edward's patronage. An engraving shows this lighthouse as a polygonal stone tower with an open platform on which a brazier provided the light source.

The light was tended by a monastic hermit who was allowed to charge light dues to pay for its upkeep. No records show how many years the light was exhibited for, but it was known to be derelict for the majority of the 16th century. Eventually, towards the end of the century, Louis de Foix, an architect from a leading royalist family, started to build a new lighthouse for King Henry III (1574–89) in 1584. He designed a lighthouse that was to be a navigation aid, chapel, and royal palace. First, he had to contend with erosion of the site, as the sea slowly reclaimed the islet. So he had to build defenses.

The work on the edifice itself was planned to take 2 or 3 years, but this was too ambitious and it was not finished until 1611. Neither de Foix nor his king lived to see the final results. Louis XIII was on the French throne by the time de Foix's assistant, François Beuscher, completed the work. The finished building was impressive by any standards.

Douglas Hague, the British expert on lighthouse architecture, described it as having "exuberant external decoration," though others—for example Fredrick Talbot, writing about it in his book *Lightships and Lighthouses* in 1913—thought the design was self-indulgent and far too grand for a lighthouse. It was also described (in several sources, including some French books on lighthouses) as the Versailles of the Sea—a reference to the Palace of Versailles near Paris, which had been converted from a hunting lodge built in 1632 for Louis XIII into a palace for Louis XIV between 1661 and 1710. Douglas Hague in his book *Lighthouses, Architecture and History*, published in 1975 gives the following description:

> The lowest or entrance stage is 161.5 metre diameter, decorated with Etruscan pilasters, which also feature in the portico. Internally, the dimly lit entrance hall is 6.7m [22 feet] square with a basement reached by small newel [winding] stairs. The main stair, which is also a newel, is nearly 27.8 metres [91 feet] in diameter, leads to the chamber above known as the King's Hall, also 6.7m [22 feet] square, which has a marble floor, vaulted ceiling and is decorated with busts of savants. Elaborate recesses lead to windows and various mural chambers and to an external observation gallery, above which the external diameter is decreased to 13 metres [43 feet]. The next stage contains perhaps the most remarkable room ever to be found in a lighthouse. The Royal Chapel 9.35 metres [31 feet] in diameter, crowned by a coffered vault 11.25 metres [37 feet] high. Three windows now light it but originally the light came from seven dormers in the dome. There are four original semi-circular niches flanked by Corinthian pilasters and the wall face is richly embellished with cartouches and swags.

By the 1780s the building was suffering from neglect and the ravages of the sea, the spit of land on which it stood being slowly eroded away. Renovations began about 1785 supervised by the architect Joseph Teulere. He removed all the old building above the Royal Chapel, and built a circular masonry tower on top with a new lantern that housed a revolving Argand reflector lamp. This increased the height to 197 feet (60 meters). The lighthouse was completed just as the French Revolution began in 1789. It did not escape the ravages of that time, and was vandalized when busts of two King Henrys placed by Louis de Foix in his tower were hurled to the ground. After the Revolution, some minor repairs were made.

Augustin Fresnel used the lighthouse for experiments

ABOVE *The wave action at Cordouan caused many problems with the foundation. The sea wall around the base was added to prevent the erosion of the sand from under the tower.*

with his lenses and in 1822 it was the first lighthouse to be permanently fitted with a Fresnel system. In spite of this pioneering work, it would seem that the structure was again neglected. This was confirmed in a letter dated August 31, 1834, written by Alan Stevenson (see Chapter 4) to his father in Edinburgh. He reported that the building was decaying and that the main central stairway was running with water after a storm, because the walls and windows leaked. He was very unhappy that the building was in such poor condition. Whether his father made representations to the French government is not known, but in 1852 the lighthouse was declared to be a historic monument and the following year arranged for the chapel to be rebuilt on the first floor, complete with stained-glass windows. Alexander George Findlay, in his *Lighthouses of the World* lists Cordouan as having a revolving bright light flashing every minute, and a secondary sectored (that is, not visible from all around) red light. He notes that it is a handsome structure, 207 feet (63 meters) high on a rock, and that focal plane of the light is 194 feet (59 meters) above mean high water. The range of the white light is given as 27 miles. Since then, a number of modernization programs have taken place. The lighthouse is still a major aid to navigation and the oldest lighthouse in operation in the world.

ABOVE *The design of this offshore lighthouse at Skerryvore is both graceful and functional. The swept out base anchors the tower firmly to its bedrock.*

RIGHT *Sections and elevations of David Stevenson's design for his lighthouses at Skerryvore, Wolf Rock, and Chicken Rock.*

LOOKS DO COUNT: STEVENSON'S LIGHTHOUSE ODYSSEY

Just how important the aesthetic aspect of lighthouse design was to the early lighthouse builders might be seen in Robert Stevenson's notes during his tours of English Lighthouses taken in the summers of 1801, 1813, and 1817. Luckily for posterity, his notes were put into a book and published in 1946 by his great-grandson D. Alan Stevenson. During these tours, Robert Stevenson visited each of the major, and some of the minor, English lighthouses. Robert was not just a casual lighthouse visitor but took the time and trouble to inspect the equipment thoroughly, commenting on its efficiency and that of the keepers tending it. He was an enthusiastic lighthouse visitor, always with the object of increasing his knowledge and making sure that he kept abreast of developments. He says very little about the design of the lighthouse building, unless he thought it affected how the lighthouse operated adversely.

During his 1801 tour, he visited the lighthouse at Douglas, Isle of Man. Here he did take notice of the design, noting, "It is an elegant structure of polished ashlar [masonry consisting of thin slabs of square stone, used for facing] erected on the head of the famous pier." Shortly afterwards, he arrived at Liverpool, to see the lighthouses used to guide ships into the River Mersey. His note about the Liverpool "sea-light" (he wrote that it was three miles northwest of the Bidston lighthouse, which would identify it as the lighthouse at Leasowe) said only that it was a "huge pile one hundred and thirty five feet high." Presumably it was a lack of architectural merit that made him appear so dismissive.

The Smalls Lighthouse (further down the Irish Sea) a few days later "deserved no better appellation than a raft of timber rudely put together." He also noted that workmen were replacing the middle pillar of the structure, which had fallen. He left the lighthouse as twilight fell, commenting that he was "rather more disappointed than pleased" with what he had seen. In an 8-week grueling schedule he visited 24 lighthouses, travelling by packet boat and by hiring small boats as he needed them.

The tours in the summer of 1813 and 1818 followed a similar pattern, his emphasis here being on the types and operation of lamps. In August 1813 in poor weather conditions he recorded how he feared for his life when going out to the Eddystone Lighthouse off southwest England in the tender, the crew of which consisted of a master, aged 70, the mate, aged "about" 65, and the deckhand, a man of 50. Robert was not satisfied with this and asked that a younger seaman be made available to help him with the small boat he would take to reach the lighthouse steps.

During the transfer, the old master and the young seaman rowed the boat, and their unequal strengths made the journey interesting to say the least—the boat was almost uncontrollable! But after some near misses, Stevenson managed to get into the tower. His notes about the boat ride offered the disdainful and perhaps rather understated observation, "I felt no small unease at being so ill-provided in a crew." Once on the lighthouse, however, he lost little time in making a thorough inspection. He checked the rock base and said that the design might have been improved by the enlargement of the base "perhaps by eight feet [2.5 meters] more to the South West, by which means the tower might have been got wholly upon the solid rock." Then he compared John Smeaton's design for the third Eddystone Lighthouse (see Chapter 3), with his own Bell Rock design, and concludes that Eddystone was "rather diminutive by comparison with the eye." He left the lighthouse to brave

High Water

Section 5th Course.

Skerryvore 1838.

Section 12th Course.

Wolf Rock 1862.

Section 6th Course.

High Wa

Chicken Rock 1869.

the trip back to Plymouth—but not without once again risking life and limb. After arriving ashore he said, "I landed with a thankful heart that I had got so safely over this trip."

These events did not deter him, for 5 days later he was landing on the Wolf Rock to give advice on the site of the proposed lighthouse there. He said of that proposal, "That it would be practicable to erect a building upon this rock I have no doubt, but from its share and figure and the great depth of water in all directions round it, together with the smallness of its dimensions, it would be a work of great difficulty, and attended with much expense and great hazard." The Wolf Rock lighthouse was finally built by James Nicholas Douglass and lit on January 1, 1870.

One of the last lighthouses Stevenson visited during his 1813 tour was the one on Flatholm Island in the Bristol Channel. He found that this one "appeared to be neatly built."

His third tour, in 1818, repeated visits to many of the sites of the first two tours. He reported more favorably on the Smalls Lighthouse, saying that it was well kept. Again, comments were made of the design of the Eddystone tower and a flying visit was also made to the Wolf Rock, though a rising tide over the rock forced a more rapid departure than he had planned. His final comments concerned the keepers' dwellings at English lighthouses. He was favorably impressed with the neatness of them.

LEFT *Europa Point lighthouse built in 1840 is a good example of a British colonial lighthouse built by the army's Corps of Royal Engineers.*

ENTER THE CIVIL ENGINEERS

The design of the lighthouses in the European countries and their colonies tended to be carried out after the middle of the 1700s by men with some training in civil engineering. John Smeaton, the constructor of the third Eddystone tower in the 1750s, was one of the first designers with formal civil engineering training to construct a lighthouse. The previous lighthouse built on the site, constructed in 1708–9, was the work of a silk merchant, John Rudyerd. Smeaton's design work included water mills, bridges, and harbors, many of which, including the upper part of his lighthouse (preserved on Plymouth Hoe) are still standing today.

The Stevensons advised on lighthouse design all over the world. Though Robert Stevenson did not attempt to visit American lighthouses, his son David made the voyage to the US in 1837 at the age of 22. He had finished his apprenticeship and traveled to America, not specifically to look at lighthouses, but to see developments in U.S. civil engineering, again, in the Stevenson manner, comparing what he saw with his own knowledge, noting the good practices and commenting adversely on the poorer ones. On his return he published a paper, *Sketches of Civil Engineering in North America*, an illustrated work mainly about the bridges and the different building materials that he encountered.

Lighthouses in the extensive empires of the British and French tended to be designed in the colony needing the lighthouse by government architects, who were also responsible for a wide range of the civil engineering works required by a developing country. The military also provided the expertise to build lighthouse. The British Royal Engineers, for instance, were responsible for a number of lighthouses, including the graceful tower that overlooks Gibraltar Strait, which they completed in 1841. The designer's name was not recorded.

Undoubtedly the greatest use of army engineers was by the United States. Many of the 592 lighthouses currently standing in the United States are a tribute to the skill and expertise of these men. It must be said that the military-designed lighthouses marked a change in U.S. lighthouse buildings from poor, second-rate towers thrown up without care to well designed, well executed structures. This dramatic change can be dated from the Congress-driven lighthouse inspection of 1850 and the setting up of the U.S. Lighthouse Board, with its membership of naval officers and army engineers.

One of the major changes was in the use of materials. Prior to 1800, most U.S. lighthouses were built of rubblestone, some of wood. Some of the better ones, such as Sandy Hook Lighthouse—built of rubblestone with a brick lining—survive to this day. Many that were lost by collapse or fire were replaced within 20 years of building. Brant Point Lighthouse, on the south shore of Nantucket Bay, suffered from both on a regular basis. The first lighthouse on the site was placed there in 1746 at the

BELOW *Port Medway lighthouse on the Nova Scotian coast is a wooden lighthouse now unmanned. Note the modern electric fog signal in front of the building in the foreground.*

ABOVE *There has been a light at Brant Point, Mass., since colonial times. The first light was built in 1759. The lighthouse pictured above is the ninth on the site.*

request of the Nantucket whaling community. It was the second lighthouse to be built on U.S. shores. It was built—or rather thrown up—of poor materials by the town, but managed, no doubt with repairs, to last 12 years before it was destroyed by fire. After a year of indecision, the town rebuilt the light in 1759, but a gale blew it down in 1774. It was either replaced or rebuilt—records do not say. The lighthouse continued to be rebuilt and destroyed—either by fire or storm—until the sixth structure on the site, erected in 1789, managed to stay in operation until 1825, when it was replaced by a lantern built on the top of the keeper's dwelling, which remains today, without its lantern. It was replaces by a new wooden tower in 1856.

Wood was still used to build the present small tower in 1901. This tower, only 26 feet (8 meters) high, is still operational and using solar power—but even that suffered some gale damage during the winter of 1991.

Sadly, the ornate wooden lighthouse built at Fort Tompkins, New York, in 1873 no longer exists. It was built with a square wooden tower topped with a glazed and copper lantern as part of a substantial wood-frame house. It was adorned with decorative iron balconies, gingerbread work, and the ornate trimmings of a well

found town house of the period. The lantern was removed in 1903 and reused at Fort Wadsworth Lighthouse, when it was established, also in 1903, overlooking the Verrazano Narrows, on Staten Island, New York.

WOOD GIVES WAY TO RUBBLESTONE

While wood was easily available and used for the smaller lighthouses, the majority of America's early towers were built using rubblestone. The construction gave them massive walls that were able to be built using any locally available stone. The stone was not dressed into shaped blocks but assembled by carefully interlocking stones of different sizes to form the wall. The accuracy of construction, and longevity of the wall, depended on the skill of the masons building it. Rubblestone walls can be many feet thick at the base, tapering with height. Weatherproofing was either by crude mortar or a lime whitewash.

Richard Devens was hired to rebuild the Boston Lighthouse at the end of the American Revolution. His instructions from the state of Massachusetts were to make it "nearly of the same dimensions of the former lighthouse." His conical structure, built in 1783, which was 75 feet (23 meters) high and 24 feet (7 meters) in diameter at the base, had walls that were 7½ feet (2.3 meters) thick at ground level.

In previous chapters we have noted the use of massive blocks of dressed quarry stone that were used to build many of the great offshore lighthouses designed by British and European lighthouse engineers. Good use was made of the granite quarried in Scotland and southwest England and shipped in vast quantities all over the world. The Fastnet Lighthouse built in 1896 off the southwest coast of Ireland used Cornish granite. Each block of close-grained, carefully selected stone weighed just over two tons and was dressed into shape using templates to make sure that each fitted into the dovetail of its neighbor. The weight of each layer of blocks secured the lower courses. To build the 88-foot (27-meter) tower, 2,074 blocks were needed, weighing 4,633, tons each of which had been shipped over 300 miles from quarry to building site.

Many U.S. lighthouses were also built in a similar way, though they usually stood away from the water and therefore did not need the same massive construction. The lighthouse at Petit Manan on the Maine coast was built in 1855 using precut granite blocks. The traditionally shaped, 119-foot (36-meter) conical tower was lined with brick and has an iron lantern, which is now fitted a modern lamp unit.

In earlier lighthouses, bricks were used mainly as linings. After 1850, however, when the expertise in brick engineering required to build tall lighthouse towers became available, bricks became more widely used on many of the lighthouses built. Bricks were relatively easy to transport over large distances. A lighthouse built at East Point, Java, in East Indies, used bricks that traveled more than 8,000 miles from a brickyard in the Netherlands, completing their journey overland in mule panniers. The tallest lighthouse in the United States, at Cape Hatteras, was built of brick in 1870. There was, however, the original lighthouse, built in 1803. This sandstone tower was some 95 feet (29 meters) tall, but, owing to coastal fog, was often unable to be seen by passing navigators. In 1853 a further 60 feet (18 meters) were added using bricks. This taller tower was still the cause of complaints of a similar nature, and so a brand-new tower adjacent to the old one was erected in the late 1860s and was eventually lit in 1870. Bricks were used to build the 196-foot (60-meter) tower of the last Cape Hatteras lighthouse, which is one of the most graceful brick towers in existence.

BELOW *Boston Light, U.S.A.*

THE AGE OF IRON

Though natural materials featured in most of the early civil engineering works, the weight-to-strength ratio of iron was understood by civil engineers and architects. Man has used iron since prehistoric times. Its use as a civil engineering material was not possible until blast furnaces came into use during the 18th century. In 1824, however, an English ironmaster, James Neilson, developed a furnace that used hot, blasted air and produced a better-quality iron for casting. From this date, the use of cast iron for lighthouses, bridges, and other major civil engineering works spread rapidly.

The first use of cast iron as a material for lighthouse towers was by the Welsh architect William Jernigan in 1803. He used locally cast material for his pier-head lighthouse at the Welsh tinplate port of Swansea. The lighthouse, a 20-foot (6-meter) octagonal tower, was cast at the Neath Abbey Ironworks about five miles away up the River Tawe. It is likely that the completed lighthouse was transported by barge down the river to the sea.

Just before this small lighthouse was made, Alexander Gordon was born in New York. In later years he would have a significant impact on the world stock of cast-iron

lighthouses. His family moved to Britain, where he attended Edinburgh University in about 1820 and would probably have been a contemporary of Alan Stevenson. After university, he joined the civil engineer Thomas Telford to gain general experience.

In 1840, Gordon developed a prefabricated cast-iron lighthouse for the British Board of Trade for use at lighthouse sites in the colonies. The first of many to be made was cast at a foundry in England and shipped out in sections to Jamaica, where it was assembled at Mordant Point. Stephen Pleasonton at the U.S. Treasury quickly adopted the idea for use in the United States. The economic advantages would have been apparent to this guardian of public purse strings.

In 1842 he designed a lighthouse lens called a holophotal lens (a type also worked on by the Stevensons). During his work with Telford he became interested in cast iron as a building material. It made for lighter structures than similar ones built of brick or stone and could be precast is many different shapes. The sections could be manufactured relatively cheaply, and shipped to sites far

BELOW *Cast Iron Lighthouses could be made in sections and taken to site for assembly by local labor. These photographs show how each section was bolted together.*

from the foundry for erection by being bolted together, using local and relatively unskilled labor.

In 1844, the first of many prefabricated cast-iron lighthouses was erected at Long Island Head near Boston and in succeeding years cast-iron towers were placed at sites all around the United States, including the Great Lakes. The last one to be built was at Pecks Ledge, CT in 1933.

The fact that cast-iron lighthouses can be unbolted and moved with relative ease has been used to effect on a number of occasions. In 1894 the tower at Hunting Island, South Carolina, was in danger from coastal erosion and was moved back away from the encroaching sea. If ever a lighthouse station suffered from bad luck, Hunting Island could claim the doubtful honor. The first tower was built in 1859, but quite what happened to it is open to conjecture. It either toppled into the sea because of erosion or was blown up during the Civil War. What we do know is that, by the end of the war, it had vanished! In 1875 the Lighthouse Board decided to re-establish the station, but to erect a cast-iron tower on a new site that was a mile from the end of the island. The 136 foot (41-meter) tower was brick-lined to insulate and stiffen it. The light was relit on July 1, 1875—but within three years the sea was within 400 feet (122 meters) of the keeper's house. A

ABOVE *Steel staircase inside Ijmuiden Lighthouse, Holland.*

LEFT *A steel lighthouse at Big Sable, Lake Michigan*

seawall was built to protect the station, but the sea continued its encroachment until by 1887, was only 60 feet (18 meters) from the buildings, with the distinct possibility that the tower's foundations would be undermined. In 1889, the tower was taken down, moved over a mile inland, and relit at the start of October the same year. The keeper's dwelling and the fog signal building, both made of timber, were demolished. The light was deactivated in 1933, but remains a good example of this type of structure.

Not all cast-iron towers were made in the traditional conical style: some of the early American offshore towers were made as a straight tube just large enough to house an access stairway to enable the keeper to climb up to the lantern. An external framework with four legs then supported this column, with its legs placed on piles driven into the mud or sand base. The advantage that this type of tower and later steel ones provided was that they

could be made of standardized sections and were lightweight. The first example, a 76 foot (23-meter) tower, was built at Whitefish Point, Michigan, in 1861. As technology developed, this design was used at greater heights. In 1895 the Cape Charles Lighthouse off the Virginia shore became the tallest of its type at 191 feet (58 meters) from its base to the top of its lantern.

THE AGE OF STEEL

Steel was used for another type of tower, the offshore caisson. These towers were again built on the shore, usually in a shipyard, and then towed out to their chosen site. The original design is claimed by an Englishman, Dr. Lawrence Potts, after his experiments in 1845, but it is known that a Frenchman, Michel Triger, had tried a similar system two years before. Potts sank a hollow metal tube to the seabed with its open end well above the sea level. He attached a large hose over the open end, with the other end attached to a powerful pump. By the drawing out of the air and water at the top, sand was drawn into the bottom. This made the tube sink into the seabed by gravity.

The idea was taken up by an American civil engineer named Charles Fox for use with railway bridges, so that he could place support columns in the soft mud of rivers and riverbanks. It was used in 1850 for the supports of the Rochester (New York) bridge, but workmen found that the sinking tube was impeded by rocks. The site engineer, James Hughes, tried to reverse the process by blowing air into the tube so that his men could be lowered to clear the obstruction, still allowing the weight of the tube to sink it into the bed. The idea worked so well that it became the accepted method of caisson tube sinking and was used on the Brooklyn Bridge and Eiffel Tower supports.

The Caisson lighthouse tower works on exactly the same principal, the only difference being the much larger diameter of tube. Though expensive to build, they are used where ice flows would damage a pile lighthouse (see Chapter 2), so are used not only in North American waters but also in the Baltic Sea. The Duxbury Lighthouse, known as the "bug," was the first one in U.S. waters in 1871, when it was towed out into Duxbury Reef in Plymouth Harbor, Massachusetts. The lighthouse, that was later seen to resemble an automobile spark plug, is made of cast iron and is only 47 feet (14 meters) high. The original light was from a fourth-order Fresnel lens with an oil lamp, but is now a modern solar-powered light.

LEFT *Steel tower at Duxbury Pier.*

The lighthouse at Sullivan's Island, Charleston, South Carolina, has a 165-foot (50-meter) tower made of steel frames covered in aluminum. It has an unusual triangular cross-section to help protect it against hurricane winds. This also contains the only elevator in a U.S. lighthouse. It replaced the old lighthouse on nearby Morris Island, which was threatened by coastal erosion.

REINFORCED CONCRETE

The Caisson lighthouse design can also be used with reinforced concrete. A number of lighthouses using the Swedish Gellerstad design (developed by Robert Gellerstad of the Swedish Lighthouse Service in 1960) are in use in European waters. The first reinforced-concrete lighthouses were built in about 1900 in Russian waters, though almost nothing was published about them. At the same time a number of lighthouse engineers were looking at the material's potential use. Lieutenant Colonel William Anderson, the chief engineer of the Canadian Lighthouse Service, was the first to use it when, in 1907, he designed Estevan Point Lighthouse in British Columbia, which was built a year later and lit in 1909. Before building could start, a railway was built from the nearest safe landing place about four miles away. The raw materials and labor force were shipped from Vancouver to the site by steam tender. Temporary wooden shuttering was erected to form a mold in the shape of the lighthouse. This mold eventually rose to a height of 150 feet (46 meters). The concrete was then poured in from buckets laboriously hoisted up the scaffolding by the construction hands. In spite of several problems—raids by local disaffected

ABOVE *The concrete tower of Point Arena Lighthouse.*

Indians who objected to their land being taken over for the lighthouse station, heavy rainfall, and damage to men and equipment—the lighthouse was completed in April 1909. The resulting lighthouse—a central tower with swept flying buttresses from just below the 25-ton iron lantern room—though a change from traditional design, was a graceful and strong building. Its success led to many others in all parts of the world. The first on American soil was built in 1908 at the Point Arena light station on the Californian coast. It replaced a temporary lighthouse that had been quickly erected following the destruction of an earlier lighthouse by the 1906 San Francisco earthquake.

Reinforced concrete has been used until quite recent times to build replacement lighthouses—the one at Cape Sarichef in Alaska in 1950, for example, where it replaced the one built in 1904, which was the only manned light on the Bering Strait.

The building of a nuclear power station near to the Dungeness Lighthouse on the south coast of England forced Trinity House to build a new lighthouse. The new building was obscuring the light from the southwest, so the replacement tower was built to the west of the old light. Reinforced concrete was chosen, and the lighthouse tower was built of 21 prestressed, circular, drum-shaped sections, each 5 feet (1.5 meter) high and 12 feet (3.5 meters) in diameter. These sections were manufactured at Rye, 12 miles from the site and delivered by low loader. A large crane lifted each interlocking section into place before

NEXT PAGE *Raz de Seine, Terenec, Brittany.*

they were held together using high-strength wires running under tension from top to base. Colored concrete was used to create a banded effect, which was achieved by alternating black and white sections. This obviated the need for painting in future years. A fog signal was also built in the tower section, which is surmounted with a conventional lantern and gallery. The last traditionally designed towers in the United States was built of reinforced concrete in 1962 at Oak Island, South Carolina.

THOROUGHLY MODERN ...

We have looked at the materials that designers have used for many years to build a wide variety of lighthouse structures. Until the 1960s, the lighthouse designer needed to allow in his design space somewhere for the keepers to live. But from that date lights could be controlled by remote devices, and keepers, though retained on some of the traditional light stations until the end of the 1990s, no longer needed accommodation.

Lighthouses are still being built, but now the designer can use modern materials. These modern designs use modern materials such as aluminum and glass-reinforced plastic (GRP), and even glass bricks as in the case of the lighthouse built on the breakwater at Takamatsu, Shikoku Island,

Japan (see Chapter 8). Some structures are in the form of a tower, some as a square box shape. In 1999, the Japanese government rebuilt many lighthouses in the Philippines. Each tower, totally self-contained and remotely operated by radio telemetry, was made of lightweight aluminum coated to protect from the effects of sunshine and salt air.

In the late 1990s, Scotland's Northern Lighthouse Board needed to improve navigation lighting on the west coast deep-water route used by oil tankers in the environmentally sensitive Minch Channel to the west of the Hebrides. Three new lighthouses were established at Hyskeir, Gasker, and the Monach Islands. From a main base at Hyskeir, workmen were ferried by helicopter to prepare the sites for the arrival of the equipment. Aluminum units were used at Gasker and the Monach Islands and a GRP tower at Hyskeir. The project to build and commission the three lighthouses took place in appaling weather conditions during the summer of 1997. The lighthouses may have been modern, but the elements and site conditions were just the same as in 1864, when David Stevenson built the original Monach Lighthouse.

BELOW *The liner Queen Elizabeth II passing the modern, reinforced-concrete tower on the end of Blankenese front light, River Elbe, Germany.*

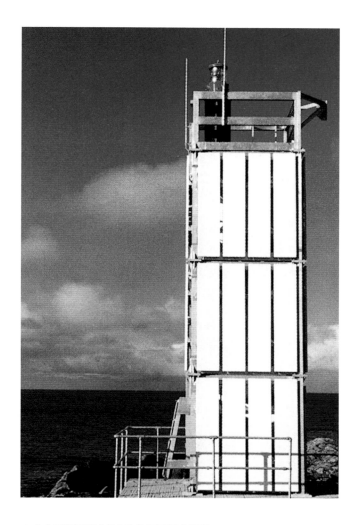

A MODERN LIGHTHOUSE

Throughout this book, we have discussed lighthouses designed and built prior to the end of the 20th century. Though the need for lighthouses in the modern maritime world has diminished, there is still a need on some coasts of the world for unlit stretches of coast to be lit.

The Spanish Costa Dorada is one example. A review of Spanish lighthouses between 1985 and 1989 determined that a new lighthouse was needed to complement those at Cape Salou and Punta San Cristóbal. The site chosen was a headland near the town of Torredembarra, situated 10 miles (6.25 kilometers) to the northeast of Tarragona. Preliminary design specifications indicated that the focal plane of the light would need to be 190 feet (58 meters) above sea level to give the required range of 17 nautical miles (19.5 land miles or 31.5 kilometers). As the proliferation of modern modular lighthouses placed on the Spanish coast in the 1960s had proved unpopular with local people and tourists, a design competition was launched, and a consultation period was allowed for environmental and technical input.

The environmentalists requested that the planned generator housing above ground should be placed underground to minimize noise and visual impact. To cater for visitors, a viewing platform was incorporated below the lantern chamber (the first time that lighthouse designers had

ABOVE, LEFT AND RIGHT *Hyskeir Major Light and Monach Isles Minor Light. Automated lighthouses built in 2000 to mark the oil tanker route off Scotland's west coast. They use modern materials — GRP and aluminium alloys.*

considered an additional use for a lighthouse rather than seeing it simply as an aid to safe navigation). The winning design, by Jose Llinas Carmona, called for a 100-foot (or, more precisely, 30.57-meter) tower constructed using reinforced concrete 15¾ inches (40 centimeters) thick. The lantern—built from forged ironwork, copper, and brass and surmounted by an ornamental weathervane—was made by the Spanish lighthouse equipment maker La Maquinista Valenciana for use during the proposed modernization of Canary Islands lighthouses in 1970, but was never used. The six-part dioptric lens system had been previously used as part of an AGA gas lamp system at another lighthouse and stored after that light was electrified. The lantern was placed on top of a massive sunshade that overhangs the viewing platform to shield the large picture windows from the sun. The light, which was ceremonially lit at midnight on January 1, 2000, is a modern dual-lamp changer using electrically powered 450-watt metal halogen bulbs and so entered the history books as the first lighthouse to be built in the 20th century and the first to be lit in the 21st.

Chapter 8 | AUTOMATION ARRIVES

For hundreds of years, the light shown by a lighthouse relied on the diligence of the keeper to ensure its maximum efficiency during the hours of darkness. He also had to ensure that the fog signal was sounded at the first signs of diminishing visibility. It was only through skilled and regular attention that the light from the early lamps burned cleanly. The large area of lantern glass had to be cleaned every day so that the output of the light was at its maximum. The revolving light required its clockwork motor to be manually wound throughout the night. Rules and regulations governed the work schedule to make sure that all these tasks were carried out. These rules also instructed the keeper on the activities required by the lighthouse authority to keep the appearance of the lighthouse station and its occupants to a high standard. It's no surprise to find that the keeper had little time left on his hands. So you can well imagine that any means of automating some of this drudgery would be a welcome innovation.

AS FAR AS LIGHTHOUSES ARE CONCERNED, automation is not a new idea. As early as 1896, Reuben Plass, an inventor and engineer, later noted for his development of motor vehicles, suggested to the U.S. government that a chain of automatic floating lighthouses should be placed at intervals of one mile across the North Atlantic, stretching from the Irish Coast to New York. They would, he postulated, be fitted with apparatus that would switch the light on at dusk and off again at dawn, and they would be fuelled for six months at a time. Ladders were to be provided so that shipwrecked persons could use the lighthouses as refuges. There would be a store of food for such emergencies, along with an unspecified device to attract the attention of rescuers. Central manned stations were to be placed every 100 miles, where crews

with rescue boats would be based. These central stations would be provided with telephones for communication by cable with the shore and each other.

Plass, from Brooklyn, New York, was not the only Victorian lighthouse figure to consider the possibilities of automated lights. What helped drive the thinking forward was the gradual replacement of fuel oils by much cleaner gas and electricity. This meant that a keeper no longer needed to spend hours cleaning away soot residue from the lantern, or trimming wicks. As soon as the light was extinguished, curtains to protect the lens system from sunlight could be pulled around the lantern.

RIGHT *The automatic light at Loop Head Lighthouse, Ireland.*

So, while taking some of the hard work and tedious routine out of a keeper's life, the advent of gas or electricity also began the process of automation—a process that would, during the hundred years from 1900, see the replacement of the keeper by a variety of automatic devices. Many ideas were tried, some successfully, and many remain in use.

Earlier, in 1881, two engineers from the Swedish Lighthouse Service, Charles Nyberg and Georg Lyth, had invented an oil lamp that burned without attention for ten days. It was improved in 1889 to burn kerosene. The lamp had by now been combined with a flashing apparatus (operated by the lamp's own heat) that had been designed by Ludwig Lindberg in 1882, and it made a reliable automatic flashing unit. It was used extensively on the leading lights of the Swedish coast and, by 1914, more than 200 were in use. They were maintained and refueled by people living nearby, who were employed as part-time attendants by the Swedish Lighthouse Department. Though these were among the smaller lights, the idea of automation had finally arrived.

The work of Gustaf Dalen, director of the AGA Company, carried forward the principle of automation. However, rather than use a liquid fuel that needed some human attendance, Dalen chose bottled gas. The use of this readily transportable fuel source—when added to Dalen's brilliant inventions of a sun valve for switching the gas on and off, a pilot light for igniting it, an automatic flashing device, and an automatic gas-mantle changer—made the keeper redundant except for minor maintenance and cleaning duties. The first lighthouse to use Dalen's automatic equipment was the Gasfeten tower light at Karlskrona on the southeast coast of Sweden. The lighthouse was built during 1904 and lit with a fixed light in the late fall of the same year. In 1906 a Dalen flasher unit was added. The light remains in service today.

LIGHTING THE PANAMA CANAL

Though a minor lighthouse in the overall scheme of things, the success of the minor Gasfeten light was noted by many lighthouse engineers, who quickly adopted the idea where they needed to place lights on inhospitable and uninhabited coastlines. Up to this point, many such places had been left lighthouse-less, because of the difficulty in maintaining equipment and keepers in such desolate spots. By the 1920s, AGA automatic lighthouses were to be found in the wastes of Labrador, on the tropical coasts of Africa, and on the southern tip of South America, where they guided ships through the tortuous channels of the Straits of Magellan.

Automatic equipment was also used in many major lighthouse projects. One notable example was the use of

LEFT *Barnegat Light, New Jersey, U.S.A.*

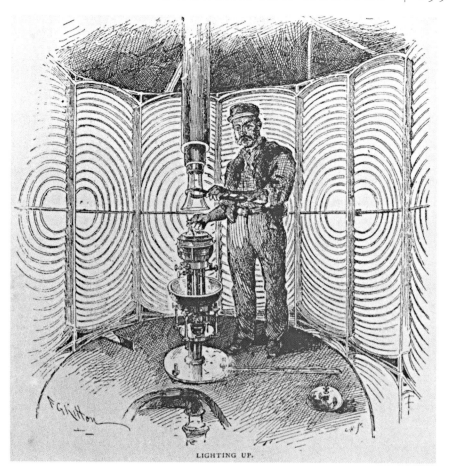

ABOVE *Compare the size of the burner and lens system with the keeper who is "putting the light in."*

AGA equipment to light the Panama Canal. This prestigious contract was acknowledged by the company as the one that saved it from financial disaster and helped it to develop into a world-renowned engineering concern.

The Panama Canal was hailed as one of the wonders of modern engineering by U.S. newspapers after the first ship passed through it in 1914. The popular slogan of the time was "The land divided, the world united!" The 50-mile-long canal linking the Atlantic with the Pacific needed to operate night and day, which meant navigational aids had to be supplied. One problem was that the canal was not cut straight across the Panamanian countryside, but followed the turns of the natural geography—this, in part, to keep the provision of expensive locks to the minimum. The AGA Company was given the lucrative contract to light the canal. It used electricity at the more accessible lights and gas for those less so. The acetylene lights were left on day and night, but the electric lights were operated at night and in poor visibility from the lock control rooms.

The lighthouses were constructed of reinforced concrete because it was thought that iron and wood might quickly deteriorate in the humid climate. All types of lighthouse design are represented along the length of the canal: landfall lights at both seaward ends to guide ships to the entrance, lights to guide them into the locks, and range lights for leads in the open parts of the waterway. Some are extremely elaborate architecturally, as exemplified by the ornate towers at Gatun Lock.

In all, AGA provided 46 lighthouses, of which 34 remain in existence. Of these, 28 are still in use, having been converted to automatic operation using photocell technology during a rolling program in the 1960s, which also controls the intensity of the output.

By the 1920s, devices patented by AGA (including the Sunvalve, an explosion-proof gas mixer, a gas-powered lens rotator, and an automatic mantle changer) had been adopted by most of the world's lighthouse authorities and designers. Sometimes, complete units were built in Sweden and shipped for erection by local contractors; in other instances,

AGA units were used as part of a designer's own system. The U.S. Lighthouse Service adopted the automatic gas light products made by AGA for many of their new lighthouse built after World War I. For example, in 1923, two automatic lighthouses were built on the Florida coast. They were placed at the Molasses Reef and at Pacific Reef to fill an unlit area between existing lighthouses at Carysfort Reef and Alligator Reef, on the chain of coral reefs to the south of the Florida coast. The lights were built on strong, open-steel frames so that they would withstand hurricane-force winds. These frames were then mounted on 8-inch-diameter (20-centimeter) wrought-iron piles driven deep into the coral. The light was a three-burner cluster in a fourth-order Fresnel lens that gave a range of 12 miles. More than 20 towers to this design were erected during the rest of the 1920s and into the 1930s (including those at Cosgrove Shoal, Smith Shoal, Tennessee Shoal, Pulaski Shoal, Benica Wharf, CA, Junes Island, MD, Olcott, NY, Upper Cedar, VA, and James Island, WA).

POWERING UP

The use of electricity, though first experimented with by the U.S. Lighthouse Service in the late 1880s, did not become common in American lighthouses until the 1920s and 1930s, when commercial power became more widely available and on-site generation was reasonably reliable.

In 1888, an attempt was made to light the Gedney Channel, an entrance channel to New York Bay. The project did not use conventional lighthouses, but marked the navigable channel with a series of spar buoys moored with weights on either side. An electric lantern was placed on each of the spars. The electric power came from a control station ashore, through six miles of cable to connect each spar light to the shore station.

The cable kept wearing out due to chafing, and the lamps and the electricity supply were not reliable, so the electric spar lights were replaced by gas-lit buoys after a few years. This did not deter continued experimentation, though, for the lighthouse engineers had seen the potential for the use of not only a clean fuel but one that meant less work for the keepers and, consequently, more economical. The south tower at Navesink Lighthouse on the northern New Jersey coast was electrified in 1899. An electric arc lamp was fitted within a bivalve-type Fresnel lens that was for many years the most powerful light on the American coast. Over the years, as needs changed, the intensity was reduced and in 1949 the U.S. Coast Guard closed down the light, because it was no longer required for navigational purposes.

LEFT *One of the twin Navesink towers on the New Jersey Coast.*

Needs change because areas are reviewed on a regular basis, and decisions on whether to downgrade or close lights down depend on whether adjacent lights have been improved, on changes in navigation channels, on comments from users, and on changing trade patterns. There has also been the modernising of ships. Sailing ships may have used a different approach to shore than a steamer, for instance, because of differences in size and shape.

STEPPING ON THE GAS

While many lighthouse engineers were beginning to see that the use of electricity was the way that lighthouse engineering would develop, in most cases technology was not advanced enough to provide the required reliability for unmanned stations.

However, the Monkstone beacon off the Welsh port of Cardiff proved more reliable. It was first placed on the Monkstone Rock in 1839 as a daymark to guide ships past a rock and shoals into safe harbor. In 1903, Sir Thomas Matthews, the chief engineer of Trinity House, designed an interesting automatic light system for the beacon. He increased its height by building housing for a reservoir to hold oil gas (gas produced from an oil base, a more modern example of which is the butane you use in a camp stove). A clockwork motor controlled the light. This drove two clocks, one to trip a switch either to open or close the gas valve during a 24-hour period, and the other to indicate the month. This second clock was necessary to adjust, by a cam and lever action, the first clock to allow for longer or shorter nights. The motor was wound automatically by a small winding device driven by the revolving lens system, which itself was driven by the gas flowing from the reservoir to the burner (ignited by a small pilot jet). It was an ingenious system that worked well and was improved in 1925, when the fuel was changed to acetylene gas and an AGA lamp was fitted. It was modernized in 1993, when an electric lamp was installed, which was powered from batteries recharged by solar energy. The iron equipment house designed by Matthews was replaced by a glass-reinforced plastic housing during the last modernization.

The use of the automatic acetylene gas and gas-oil systems was not confined to lighthouses. There were many successful applications on buoys and lightvessels. The development in the 1890s of the acetylene-powered buoy by Thomas Willson in Canada has already been noted in Chapter 3. The Stevenson brothers, David and Charles, designed what they termed gas lightboats. This type of floating light became known as the Otter Rock type, after the brothers' first attempt to use one, to mark the Otter Rock in 1901. This was an outlying rock off the southern

ABOVE *An unmanned automatic LANBY (Large Automatic Navigation Buoy). This example is on the OWERS station off the south coast of England, but the design is used all over the world.*

end of the Hebridean island of Islay. The lightboat, whose light was placed on a lattice tower to keep it clear of the sea, was also fitted with a fog bell. The bell had two clappers. One was operated by wave motion when the vessel rolled, but it was soon realized by the designers that fog occurs in periods of flat calm, and so a second clapper was fitted. This was powered by the gas supply to the light. The gas was diverted through a receiver containing a flexible diaphragm. As this was forced upward, it activated a linkage that caused the clapper to strike the bell. The returning clapper pushed the diaphragm down, expelling the gas charge to the lamp.

During foggy weather, the light flashed and the bell sounded in unison. Unfortunately, though this automatic system was successful, the lightfloat broke away from its

NEXT PAGE *East Brothers Light Station, San Francisco Bay.*

moorings and was stranded on a local beach during a winter storm in 1902. The lightboat was badly damaged but salvaged, dry-docked, repaired, and returned to station.

During the early years of the twentieth century, Scotland's Northern Lighthouse Board began to use Otter Rock-type lightboats at similar stations in the Hebrides and the Isle of Man, while the Imperial Lighthouse Service ordered a large number for use in the river deltas of India and Burma (now Myanmar). They were also used off the Australian coast. Vessels of the same generic type were also made by the AGA Company, who supplied them to ports throughout the world.

Gas was used off one of the Channel Islands, too. General Campbell, the governor of Guernsey, was petitioned in the early 1900s by the shipping companies that used the Little Russel Channel when approaching St. Peter Port, the island's capital. The channel is rock-strewn, with fierce cross tides and rips and a tendency to fog and mist. They wanted a light and fog signal placed on the Platte Fougere rock, which would mark the entrance. Campbell decided to approach the Stevensons for advice and a plan of a possible lighthouse. They had considerable experience with similar problems off the Scottish coast. After a detailed survey of the site, they proposed that they should be contracted to build a combined light and fog-signal station on the rock. It was to be unmanned and semi-automatic in operation with control from a keeper's station at Fort Doyle, which is on Guernsey and about a mile from the rock.

The tower they built was called the ugliest lighthouse in Britain by a lighthouse historian of the time, Frederick Talbot. Unlike their normally graceful stone towers, the one proposed by the Stevensons was an 80-foot (25-meter) ferro-cement affair that was an irregular octagon shape. This form, they reasoned, would provide less resistance to the force of the currents by easing the pressure of their flow on the base of the structure. The solid base of the tower rises 46 feet (14 meters) above the rock. On this firm base they continued the structure, but built in compartments for equipment. Each of the lower two contained an electrically driven compressor for the fog signal—one for use and one for standby in case the first failed. In the top of the tower they placed an acetylene-making plant and an automatic AGA gas light, the air receivers (large steel tanks that hold compressed air), and the fog siren and its trumpet. A clockwork timer operated the light. The fog signal, however, was turned on and off from the control point ashore. A house for the keepers and an engine house were built, the latter to hold the two sets of electricity-generating equipment and the compressor for a land-based auxiliary fog signal. The land-based signal was felt to be a necessary in the event that the one out on Platte

LEFT *Phare de la Jument, Brittany, France.*

Fougere failed. The land station was connected to the lighthouse by a massive, specially made, armored cable. This double-sheathed cable was 3.5 inches (90 millimeters) in diameter and weighed about 45 tons. This was carefully laid on the seabed. The multicored cable had three wires: one for carrying electricity to the electric motor, a telephone cable, and a control wire. The control wire operated an electric switching device to select and start the air-compressor motors as soon the duty keeper saw fog. When the keeper activated the fog signal, it sounded, the compressor began to replace the air in the storage tank, and a bell rang in the shore control room. The keeper heard the fog signal some five seconds later. If the fog signal failed, the bell rang continuously to warn him. He then started the auxiliary fog signal ashore.

The description of this semi-automatic station would not be complete without reference to the device designed by the Stevensons to "automatically" keep the duty keeper alert and on fog watch. There was an electric alarm next to the keeper, silent as long as he pressed a register switch at regular intervals. If he fell asleep or left his post, an alarm sounded to call the off-duty keeper to the control room. There is no record of the time allowed for the duty man to visit the bathroom! When this structure was built in 1910, the cost was £8,500 ($42,000). The Stevensons noted that a conventional manned tower on the same site would have cost £60,000 ($300,000).

ENTER PETROLEUM

In some parts of the world such as the vastness of the Australian coast and shores of Far Eastern countries, calcium carbide, the raw material for making acetylene gas, was not readily available, but petroleum gas was abundant almost worldwide. The Wigham Company, based in Dublin, Ireland, developed what they christened the Thirty-One-Day light in the late 1890s. Although so called, it was able, with a larger fuel supply, to operate unattended for longer periods. One that they supplied for the Manora breakwater light at Karachi, Pakistan, was set up to operate for 100 days at a stretch during the monsoon season.

The method of operation was unusual. The lamp was made in three parts. The top was a lenses unit housing the burner. Below this was the reservoir that held the wick and its fuel. The wick itself took the form of a flat "conveyor

RIGHT *The magnificent Hyper-radial lens weighing 15 tons and standing over twenty feet (6.06 meters) high. Built by Chance Bros, Bormingham, England for installation at Manora Point Lighthouse, Pakistan. Hyper-radial Lenses with a 52 inch (1330 mm) focal length were the largest lenses ever built.*

belt." This meant that the flame burned on the flat of the wick rather than the wick end, which otherwise would have soon deteriorated as a result of carbonization. The wick was hooked to a weighted float in a second reservoir below the fuel reservoir. The oil from the second reservoir was allowed by a micrometer valve to drip away very slowly. As the level of oil in this reservoir dropped, the float slowly sank and, in doing so, dragged the wick through its fuel bath and onto the burning platform under the lens.

This type of light was developed further using multiple wicks to give a more powerful light and had the added advantage that it was robust and could be transported to remote locations, sometimes by mule. The fact that the light was so sturdy meant that it could also be utilized as the light on board unmanned lightfloats. The British Admiralty favored this type of craft in their purpose built naval harbors. They were easy to maintain and the Admiralty always had fuel readily available. One was used very successfully in the entrance to Queenstown (now Cork) harbor, where—though lashed by stormy seas with the light washed over by the sea on occasion—it remained working.

LEFT *Taking the keepers job away. The introduction of the automatic lamp changer but using large 1000 watt filament lamp bulbs.*

RIGHT *A Trinity House keeper fitting new lamp bulbs to the automatic lamp changer at Flamborough Lighthouse, England.*

BELOW *Two styles of low-voltage, high-output halogen lamps. The three lamps in the lower right photograph replaced one of the single lamps in the lamp changer at left.*

All the various types of light that we have looked at so far used liquid fuel and flame for the light, and, although they were largely successful, designers still had problems with getting very bright lights. Although the use of electricity had been tried in the middle of the ninteenth century, it had not been very successful (see Chapter 3). The development of filament-lamp technology and the ability to store low-voltage electricity in batteries slowly changed the techniques of lighthouse automation.

IT'S A GENERATION THING

While the major lighthouses remained manned using Hood or Kitson burners with kerosene fuel, the way for their automation was being paved by work at some of the smaller coastal lights. The change from kerosene to electric light was quite slow. Not many lighthouses were close enough to a commercial power supply, so electricity had to be generated on the spot using either gasoline- or diesel-driven generators. The first machines were not particularly reliable and thus needed the care and attention of keepers to work and produce electricity efficiently.

Because an electric light is about ten times as bright as a kerosene one, once the filament bulb's reliability had been established, the light source was able to be much smaller and the changeover from oil- and gas-fired lighthouses began

in earnest. By the mid-1920s, electricity was in general use in the U.S.A. and urban areas had their own generating stations. Where lights were situated close to a commercial power supply, lighthouse engineers took advantage of the electricity and conversion the stations. During the prewar period the majority of U.S. lighthouses became electrified. Where commercial power was not available, gasoline or diesel generators provided the power. Though at first the keepers merely changed from being lamplighters to engine drivers, it was not long before methods of switching the lights on and off automatically were introduced.

In 1935, two American engineers, Wallace and Tiernan, began to develop automatic time switches and automatic lamp changers. The lamp changers were simple rotating turrets that held spare bulbs. When the in-service bulb burned out, the electrical circuitry in the device would sense that there was no current, and this would be its signal to

BELOW LEFT *Each lamp bulb will have a life exceeding 2000 hours.*

BELOW *No keeper needed! The rotating turret changes the bulb as each one fails*

RIGHT *Keeepers eye view from the Lantern room, The lens is a first order lens.*

cause the lamp changer to rotate, bringing a new lamp bulb into position. The early electrically driven automation equipment was still based on mechanical operations rather than the electrical devices of the post-World War II years.

During the years following World War II, there were many lighthouses that had been damaged during the conflict, and others that, owing to wartime economies, had not been maintained as they would have been in peacetime. The American offshore lighthouse at Minot's Ledge off Boston was one such. It was built in 1850 and was fitted originally with a third-order Fresnel lens and an Argand lamp. The lamp was replaced during the 1900s by a pressurized kerosene vapor burner (I.O.V) and tended by a crew of keepers until 1947. In that year the lighthouse was electrified and automated, and the keepers' places were taken by automatic, on-site control using continuously operating diesel-powered generators. In 1983 the generators were replaced by a solar-powered, 11.8-inch (300-millimeter), battery-operated lamp.

Slowly but surely, all U.S. lighthouses were automated, and lightships were replaced by buoys or fixed steel towers. By the end of the 1960s, the only lighthouse still manned by the United States Coast Guard was the one on Little Brewster Island, Boston. Keepers have looked after it since 1789, and will always do so, unless the Act of Congress requiring the permanent presence of keepers is repealed.

ACROSS THE SEA TO IRELAND

Although in the 1960s, in many parts of the world, keepers were being removed and trust was placed in automatic equipment, the Commissioners for Irish Lights, based in Dublin, decided that their new lighthouse on the Kish Bank in Dublin Bay would have keepers. The lighthouse was to be built on the busy ferry route into Dublin, and this swayed the commissioners' decision to replace the lightship that had been stationed on the sandbanks since 1811.

The commissioners decided to use a construction concept developed by Robert Gellerstad of the Swedish Lighthouse Service in 1960, which would be suited to this type of seabed. The novel idea was a floating structure that opened like a telescope, which could be built onshore, launched, and towed to its site completely fitted out and ready to operate.

There were already 34 of these lighthouses in service in the Baltic, but Kish Bank was to be the largest of its type to be attempted. At Dun Laoghaire, a small port just south of Dublin, work began in 1962 to build the base, which was a ferro-concrete caisson-type structure. As we have seen with

LEFT *Start Point Lighthouse on the Devonshire coast in southern England.*

ABOVE *Trinity House Light Vessel No 19 on an unusually calm day on its station off the Isles of Scilly, U.K. The helipad allows technicians to board the vessel and carry out maintenance, as the vessel is unmanned.*

earlier lighthouse builders, the weather was always a factor to be considered. Gale-force winds in May 1963 gave the builders major problems when the winds wrecked the partially built structure. The damage was made good and construction proceeded until the lighthouse could be launched into the bay in November 1964. The 7,000-ton structure was then completely fitted with its lantern, engine rooms, and keepers' quarters. It was ready to be towed to site by the following June.

However, gales again caused problems and the lighthouse was deliberately grounded on one of the bay's sandbanks close to its intended site until the weather improved. It was then placed in position by flooding special honeycomb compartments in its base (the water acting as a temporary ballast). To hold it in place the floodwater was replaced by sand. The next stage was for the main tower, which was inside the caisson, to be lifted into position. This was done by pumping water underneath it so that it was lifted hydraulically and then secured in place, the water again being replaced by sand. As soon as the lighthouse was in place, a team of keepers were flown in by helicopter, the generators were started, and the light was lit. It ceased to be a manned station in 1995, when the light was automated

and controlled from the shore monitoring station at Dun Laoghaire depot.

The lighthouse authorities in Britain as elsewhere in the world had retained the pressurized-vapor burner in manned offshore lights, but by the middle of the 1970s the program to automate all lighthouses, including those offshore, by the end of the twentieth century was well under way. The land stations such as Strumble Head on the Welsh coast and Start Point on the South Devon coast of England were automated, demanned, and left with an attendant who visited on a regular basis to clean and check over the station. The unmanned stations became part of a group controlled by a land station that remained fully staffed by a team of keepers who monitored the status of the stations in their group by computer via telephone or a radio-telemetry link. In 1982 Trinity House automated the famous Eddystone Rock lighthouse off Plymouth, England, which was their first offshore station to be operated using automatic equipment and monitored from the shore.

In Chapter 6 we saw how helipads built on the tops of the lanterns of the offshore lights had made the changeover of keepers much easier. Now, in the days of automation, this ease of access in almost any weather also made the task of emergency visits by helicopter-borne technicians faster to organize, so that any malfunctioning equipment reported by the monitor station could be repaired very quickly. The automation process also covered for the possibility of failure of equipment because it allowed duplication.

MODERN AUTOMATION OF LIGHTHOUSES

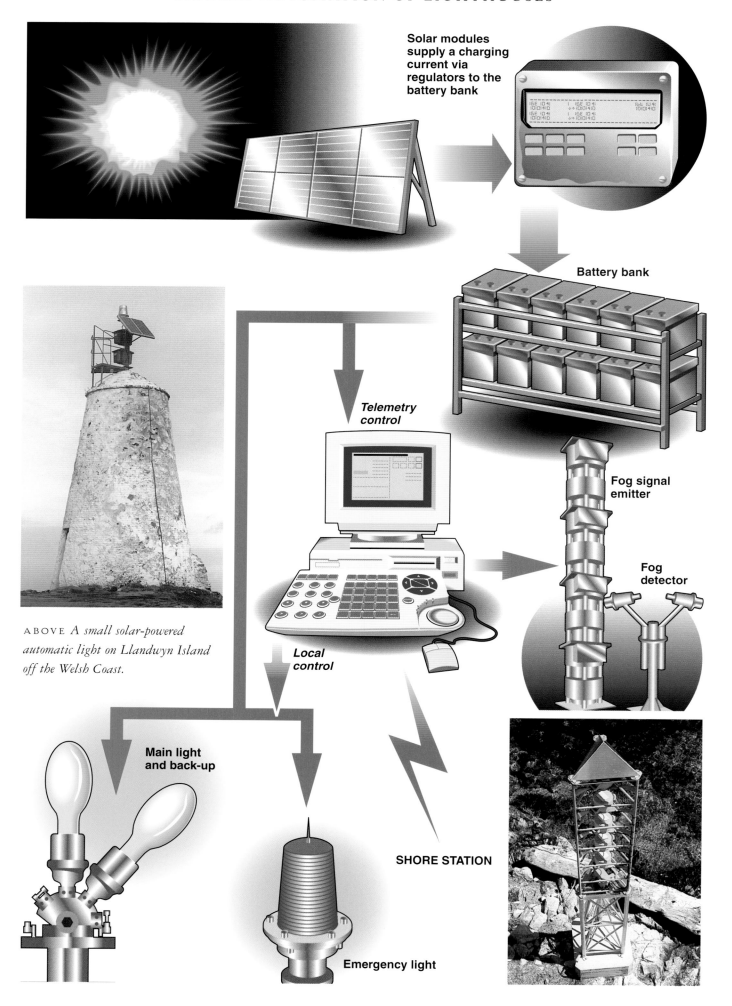

Solar modules supply a charging current via regulators to the battery bank

Battery bank

Telemetry control

Fog signal emitter

Fog detector

Local control

ABOVE *A small solar-powered automatic light on Llandwyn Island off the Welsh Coast.*

Main light and back-up

SHORE STATION

Emergency light

Just as with lighthouses, the new technology enabled lightships also to be demanned. As we have seen, small automatic lightboats had been successfully used since the early 1900s. The number of lightships with crews onboard to operate them had fallen as the second half of the twentieth century dawned. On some stations, the new automatic buoys were able to take the place of an expensive lightship; other lightships were withdrawn because of a change in shipping activity in their area. The United States Coast Guard, where they did not use an automatic buoy, replaced the lightship with a Texas Tower (see Chapter 6). Trinity House in British waters were one of the few lighthouse authorities to continue to use lightships, though their fleet of 55 ships had been downsized to ten by the early 1990s.

PREVIOUS PAGE *Trinity House helicopter, "Lima Sierra," delivering stores to Eddystone lighthouse using the underslung load method of transferring cargo from tender to lighthouse.*

A GUIDING LIGHT FOR NEW YORK

The Ambrose Lightship station off New York is a typical example of the progression in American waters from manned ship to automated tower. The Ambrose station was the site of the 1823 Sandy Hook lightship mentioned in previous chapters (the name was changed in 1908 to honor Dr. John W. Ambrose, who was credited with persuading the U.S. government to dredge what is now known as the Ambrose Shipping Channel). Lightships on this station were used by the lighthouse administration to introduce innovative ideas. In 1894 it was the first station to have a lightship exhibiting an incandescent light, followed in 1921 by a lightship with the world's first radio beacon. In 1967, they replaced the lightship with a tower, with a crew of six living on it.

BELOW *The 2000 ton floating crane, "Noble Lifter," lifting the 200 foot high Inner Dowsing Lighthouse at Lowestoft Harbor.*

The tower was a substantial steel platform standing in 74 feet (23 meters) of water. The light was 136 feet (41 meters) above sea level. On the platform, there was crew accommodation, a watch room, and a 70-by-70-foot (21-by-21-meter) helicopter landing pad. The tower displayed a 10-million candlepower light, sounded a fog warning signal in low visibility, and sent out its identifying radio beacon transmission. In 1967, the tower was converted to automatic operation and, when the crew were withdrawn, the era of manned offshore lights ended in American waters.

The now automatic tower safely served the ships transiting the busy Ambrose Channel until one of them collided with the tower, almost destroying it. In November 1996 the 744-foot (227-meter) crude-oil tanker *Aegeo* hit the structure, shearing off one of its 36-inch-diameter (92-centimeter) steel supporting legs. Subsequent surveys showed that the tower, now almost 30 years old, was beyond economic repair. Emergency repairs were carried out while a new tower was planned and built.

The U.S. Coast Guard took the opportunity to both modernize the equipment and update pilotage requirements because of changes in shipping activity in the channel. The size of the modern lighting equipment and its control gear, coupled with the fact that crew accommodation would not be needed, allowed the designers to plan a much smaller tower than the one it was replacing. The new structure, built by a Louisiana-based oilrig fabricator, Offshore Specialty Fabricators, is an 80-foot (24-meter) steel tower supported by steel tripod legs. It was sited a mile and a half further out to sea in 95 feet (29 meters) of water. To ensure that the tower stayed in position, 48-inch-diameter (122-centimeter) steel piles were driven 175 feet (53 meters) into the seabed. The lighting, fog signal, racon, and control equipment are powered by 12-volt batteries, which are recharged by an array of solar panels. The main light is switched on and off by a photocell. Should the bulb fail an automatic lamp change takes place; if that fails the emergency lantern is activated. The fog signal is permanently on, sounding every 15 seconds; should it fail, a standby signal takes over immediately. The new tower, which was built at Houma, Louisiana, was transported 1,700 miles by barge. It was lifted into place on September 18, 1999, by a 500-ton-capacity floating crane. The position of the tower was accurately determined using Differential Global Positioning equipment.

A Coast Guard team fitted the automatic equipment, which was lit on September 21, 1999. The old tower was demolished and the new tower placed, which carries on the 177-year tradition of providing a guiding mark at the entrance to New York. (There was one recent interruption to this excellent service when, in January 2001, a ship hit the Ambrose Tower and temporarily put out the light.)

In European waters, all lightships have been replaced by unmanned lights, either large automatic buoys or the types of tower mentioned earlier. In British waters, both Trinity House and the Commissioners for Irish Lights have kept a small number of their lightships, which have been converted to automatic operation. The engineers working for both authorities at first automated their lightships by fitting them with radio monitoring instrumentation that enabled them to operate without their crews, but much in the same way as when they were manned. The diesel generators were run continuously to provide the electricity to light the lamp. The monitoring equipment sent status reports to a control station situated at a lighthouse ashore, and the operator at the shore station was able, if equipment failed, to send a signal to the lightship to start up a standby unit.

These ships were designated "Automatic Light Vessels" (with the initials ALV) and served on the remaining stations such as Goodwin Sands. Trinity House engineers were not content with this method, however, and were already experimenting with the use of solar power. They converted LV 95, which had been in service since 1938, first into an unmanned vessel and then into an ALV. It was the first major lightship to operate entirely by solar power. It was completely overhauled and fitted with arrays of solar panels, 90 in all, that charged banks of batteries which supplied power for the light, fog signal, and monitoring equipment. The light unit was a low-powered, 360-millimeter (14-inch), rotating optic specially designed and built by Trinity House engineers for the project. It used proven parts that were already in use in automated lighthouses, and a buoy light as an emergency backup. The fog signal was controlled by a fog detector, thus saving battery power in periods of clear weather. A GPS-based monitoring arrangement completed the control system so that the monitoring station at Harwich could not only check the integrity of the light and fog signal, but could also ensure that the ship was on its correct station. The lightship was placed in service on the Inner Dowsing station of eastern England's Lincolnshire coast, in July 1995 and proved successful. The remaining lightships in the fleet were all converted as they became due for major refit.

And so, during the 100 years of the process of automation, just as the traditional materials of stone, iron, and glass have been discarded for modern plastics, the mechanical devices to make the lights and fog signals operate have given way to solid-state electronics. The burning of oil and gas, whether directly in the lamp or in the generator engine, has given way to free energy from the sun. The constant diligence of the keeper has been replaced by the occasional visit by an attendant or maintenance technician. Some say this is for the worse, but the reliability of the lights is still assured.

Chapter 9 | TOURISM, CONSERVATION, AND PRESERVATION

As we saw in the previous chapter, the process of automation during the last century slowly but surely removed the need for lighthouse keepers. The development of satellite technology that assisted the monitoring of remote stations and global positioning equipment, and now enables lighthouse authorities to know exactly whether their floating aids to navigation are on station, has sounded the death knell for lighthouses. The reason is quite simple. Anyone, not just mariners, can now go to their local electronics store and, for less than $100, purchase a "user-friendly" Global Positioning System (GPS) instrument that will tell them where they are on the earth's surface with enough accuracy for all normal use.

THE PROFESSIONAL MARINER AND the pleasure-boat owner with a larger budget can buy and install a chart plotter, which, when combined with GPS, will show them exactly where they are in relation to their intended route, and any dangers they might encounter along the way. They no longer need the guidance of a lighthouse by day or night.

We have seen that lighthouses are paid for in many parts of the world by the imposition of light dues on the ships that use the lights. Now that ships do not need the lighthouses, there is a growing commercial pressure on the lighthouse authorities to reduce or even cease to charge dues. The modern automatic lamp in its acrylic housing stuck on a pole may be very economical to operate, but a similar lamp in a 200-year-old masonry tower, while economical in its operation alone, will actually cost much more because its surroundings are expensive to maintain. The economic fact is that, without revenue from light dues, lighthouse operators will be unable to maintain the lights in the traditional towers unless they find ways of raising revenue by alternative and complementary use of the buildings for profit.

Fortunately, the problem is not new and has been addressed by some of the major lighthouse-owning authorities during the last 20 years. As lighthouses have become redundant—and some, sadly, have been demolished by being bulldozed or simply pushed over cliffs—others have been given, sold, or leased for use as homes, museums, and heritage centers. This chapter tells the story of the successes and the failures. But first let's explore the early days of lighthouse visiting, for, as we shall learn, it is by no means a recent leisure activity.

RIGHT *The redundant lighthouse, in the center of the town of Harlingen, The Netherlands, has been converted into luxurious vacation apartments.*

OPEN HOUSE

At the end of the nineteenth century, Ella Luick was the keeper's wife at Sand Island Lighthouse, a single-family-operated station on a small island near the Wisconsin shore of Lake Superior. The nearest town, Bayfield, was about 20 miles away along the shore of the lake. This did not stop visitors to the lighthouse, however! Ella recorded in her diary for Monday, 28th August 1899, that "the yacht *Stella* arrived with a party of 14 to visit the station"; and the entry for Sunday, 17th September, records that the tug *Eliza* arrived from Bayfield.

> She had on board 10 people from Bayfield and Mr. and Mrs. Johnston of Chicago. They brought their lunch baskets up to the house and made tea in the kitchen and also ate their dinner in the kitchen. Mr. Johnston had never seen pine growing before, and was nearly wild to pick blackberries, raspberries and blueberries.

She does not say whether they visited the tower, but obviously the lighthouse visit was a highlight for Mr. Johnson, a city dweller. Lighthouse visiting was, and indeed still is, a delight for thousands of people throughout the world.

The instructions from Trinity House in Britain (no longer applicable now there are no keepers) used to be that that visitors should be allowed, but only after 12 noon and up to one hour before sunset. No visits were allowed on Sundays. The keeper was also instructed that he must greet

BELOW *Light at Sand Island, Lake Superior.*

visitors courteously and must be in full uniform. No gratuities were to be accepted—though if coins happened to fall into the keeper's upturned hat, which he had casually placed by the door ...

Many lighthouses held "open days," when, with all the brasswork gleaming and the lantern and its optic sparkling, the uniformed keepers would welcome the local people to see their pride and joy. The visitors would be allowed to climb the stairway to the lantern room—and some of the younger keepers might feel that the young ladies visiting were in need of extra personal assistance!

This tradition continues in modern times. Attendants open lighthouses for just one day during the year.

When the attendant at Strumble Head Lighthouse on the Welsh coast opened his premises for the first time in many years in July 2000 he was in for a surprise. He expected about 50 people and was amazed to count more than 500 coming through his door. Vacationers and local people braved rain, crossed a footbridge over a windswept gorge, and climbed 150 steps so that they could look round his light.

Yet that was just a small number compared with the visitors to some lighthouses in the United States. Back in 1936 records showed that 6,000 people visited the Cana Island Lighthouse on the shore of Lake Michigan—a high number, considering its isolation and the fact that there was no public transport over a dirt trail through the forest.

During the early 1990s, an agreement was made between the U.S. Coast Guard and the Oregon Bureau of Land Management for the Yaquina Head Lighthouse, first lit in 1873 on the Oregon coast, to become part of the Yaquina Head Nature Area. The lighthouse and its nearby oil store were restored and in 1994, the first year that it was opened to the public, 56,000 people visited it.

On the opposite side of the Pacific Ocean on the coast of Victoria, Australia, the lighthouse at Cape Otway overlooking the Bass Strait is one of the state's major tourist attractions. The lighthouse is leased from the Australian Maritime Safety Administration by a private company, who have developed the lighthouse and its surrounding area for tourism. Some 70,000 visitors every year experience the maritime heritage, wildlife, and natural beauty surrounding the station—Cape Otway National Park. They can visit the light tower built in 1848, when it was the first light on mainland Australia, and see the Chance Brothers' lens unit installed in 1891, which replaced the original parabolic reflector lamps. The grounds contain extensive historical buildings, including keepers' dwelling (it was a three-family station) and the 1859 building that housed the first telegraph operators. Now the homes are available for overnight visitors, while the telegraph station is soon to become a museum. Visitors can hear stories about the hundreds of shipwrecks in the area, including that of the *Cataraqui*, the worst in Australia's history, and may even chance upon koala bears or wallabies that frequent the grounds after dark.

SURPLUS TO REQUIREMENTS

In different parts of the world, the lighthouse administrations look at their stock of lighthouse buildings in different ways. The United States Coast Guard, after declaring lighthouse buildings surplus to requirements, offer them first to other government agencies, and then, if there are no takers, they are offered to staff, county, local municipality and finally a non-profit preservation group. Most of them—and certainly where aids to navigation are involved—are not disposed of, but are the subject of management and leasing agreements.

More than half of the U.S. lighthouse stock of 406 lighthouse stations are now open to the public. Many of the buildings are leased to the National Park Service; sometimes the grounds only are available, but in some cases the buildings house a small museum to display obsolete and unused equipment.

The lighthouse on the infamous prison island of Alcatraz in San Francisco Bay may not be as well known as its near neighbor, the prison itself, but an initiative by the U.S. National Park Service has ensured that it is an important part of the island's status as a National Park. Visitors are reminded by visual aids that the lighthouse site was the first on the West Coast when established in 1854. The present tower—84 feet (26 meters) high, and still operated by the Coast Guard—was built of reinforced concrete in 1909 to replace the original. Though the tower and its current lighting equipment are not open to visitors, they can see a fourth-order Fresnel lens, which served in the tower, in the prison museum.

Pigeon Point Lighthouse, also in the San Francisco Bay area, is also still active, though its lens is now a 24 inch (60 centimeter), modern aero-beacon (such as you see when you land at an airport) on the lighthouse gallery, which needs very little attention from Coast Guard technicians. The complex of buildings that surround the traditionally shaped 115-foot (35-meter) conical tower are now operated by the American Youth Hostel Organization with daily public access to the surrounding grounds. The tower is open to visitors at weekends through a state-sponsored non-profit group. The lighthouse was established on the site in 1871 and retains in its lantern its original first-order Fresnel lens.

RIGHT *The Lighthouse on Alcatraz Island, now a major tourist attraction in San Fransisco Bay.*

The lighthouse at the Kennedy Space Center in Florida, built in 1848, has the rare distinction of being managed by the U.S. Air Force. Because of its proximity to the Space Center, it is not open to the public, but its managers ensure that this interesting construction, with its steel plates, is well maintained. A new cast-iron tower, 150 feet (46 meters) high, was built in 1868, but erosion meant that the Lighthouse Board had to dismantle it, move it 1.25 miles westward and re erect it. This was in 1893–94 and it remains in that same position today.)

Down the coast, the Florida Department of Natural Resources own Cape Florida Lighthouse, the oldest surviving lighthouse in the state, having been built in 1825. The light had long periods when it was unlit and was extinguished for 10 years between 1836 and 1846 (because the threat from the Seminole still existed) and then for 100 years from 1878, until the Coast Guard fitted an automatic 1930s-type drum lens. (The 100-year gap came about because, in 1878, the new lighthouse at Fowey Rocks superceded it. The U.S. Coast Guard re-established it in 1978 after requests from the local boating community.) The lighthouse is now part of a historic recreation area.

Many lighthouses in the United States are in nature conservation areas and the keepers' dwellings are occupied by naturalists, rangers, and visitors. The Matinicus Island Lighthouse of Abigail Burgess fame is now a research facility for the biologists of the U.S. National Audubon Society. The island, with its buildings, boat-landing facilities, and helipad, is a seabird-nesting site of national importance. The Coast Guard maintains the automatic light.

Although national and state interests make up most of the alternative use of lighthouses, many community initiatives have saved their local structures. Sometimes the local town has taken the responsibility for the lighthouse and sometimes a preservation society has been formed. The local community in the town of Vinalhaven, Maine, leased their Browns Head Lighthouse from the Coast Guard after it was automated in 1987. They now use the 1832 building as a residence for their town manager.

PRESERVATION—A GROWING CONCERN

The number of lighthouse preservation societies in the U.S. is also on the increase. The leading organization is the United States Lighthouse Society, which was founded in 1984, now has more than 11,000 members. It started by declaring four aims:

LEFT *Pigeon Point Lighthouse, California, U.S.A.*

RESTORATION OF ROSE BLANCHE

The story of the Rose Blanche Lighthouse on the southwestern tip of Newfoundland shows how the tenacity of the local community has led not only to the restoration of a derelict lighthouse, but has used the project for the economic good of the community. The lighthouse was built of locally quarried granite in 1872 and fitted with a Stevenson lantern and optic made in Scotland and shipped to the site. The light was fully manned and operational until it was decommissioned and abandoned in 1949, when a lighthouse on nearby Caines Island replaced it.

The tower was left to the elements and the work of vandals until 1988, when the local tourist development association identified it as a possible tourist attraction. A plan was drawn up, funding was gained to begin restoration, and local people were trained to carry out the work.

After 12 long years of toil, and despite frustration at lack of funding—the lighthouse was finally restored. The lack of a road out to the site during the restoration program meant that all materials and equipment had to be delivered by boat or transported over rough land, so—once the lighthouse fabric had been rebuilt—the project also involved building a road and parking lot ready for the tourists. Although this was completed, funding had run out, threatening to delay completion of the roofing and paying for a suitable lens unit to display in the new lantern house. The Canadian Coast Guard came to the rescue with a Fresnel lens and funds to finish the project were finally raised from an organization called the Atlantic Ground Fish Strategy.

The restored lighthouse was given the Manning Award for Excellence in the Preservation of Historic Sites by Newfoundland's Lieutenant Governor. On 23rd July, 1999, the fully restored lighthouse was opened to the public.

THE ECLIPSER

The machinery and mechanisms used in past times are just as important as the fabric of the lighthouses. Not just the magnificent lenses but devices that showed the ingenuity of the early designers are all of interest. A wonderful example of an "eclipser"—a device that works much as its name suggests, by blocking the light at intervals—is on display at the Point Pinos Lighthouse on California's Monterey Peninsula. The eclipser was fitted when the lighthouse, built in 1855, was modernized in 1912. The intricate clockwork system driven by falling weights caused a copper shield to revolve around a continuously burning oil-vapor lamp so that the light was shown for 20 seconds and shielded for 10. The eclipser worked every night for 28 years, with a variety of light sources, before an electrically operated flasher unit replaced it.

It remained as a standby until the 1950s when it was discarded and dumped in the lighthouse grounds. In 1997 a group of volunteers found it and restored it for public display. The restoration took over 300 hours of careful work, some missing parts having to be specially manufactured. The fully restored piece is now in the basement of the lighthouse, where visitors are able to see working demonstrations.

THE STORY OF ELBOW REEF

Lighthouse building and artifact preservation are not the prerogative of the larger countries. The Elbow Reef lighthouse, now operated by the Bahamas Lighthouse Preservation Society, deserves a special place in the world lighthouse heritage because it is home to the world's last operational kerosene-fuelled light. The original light was an oil lamp, but this was upgraded to a pressure-vapor burner when the present Chance lighting equipment was installed in 1934.

In the latter half of the 1990s, the lighthouse owners, the Bahamas Port Department, planned to convert the lighthouses at Elbow Reef, San Salvador, and Great Inagua to automatic lights as part of an economy drive. The community at Hope Town near the Elbow Reef Lighthouse fought this proposal and negotiated with the Port Department. It was eventually agreed that the light could remain manually operated if the Hope Town Department of Works was responsible for its operation and upkeep.

The Bahamas Lighthouse Preservation Society became involved and assisted with locating spares. The incandescent mantle material, for example, was obtained from the Coleman Company at Wichita, Kansas, in tube form and made into mantles by a member. A contact was made with the Massachusetts Institute of Technology, who offered help with hand-made burner hardware. The tower and the lantern were painted in 1995 by the Shepard family from Florida, who were offered a "free vacation" in return for the paint job—their normal work being painting bridges and high buildings! Resplendent with its red and white stripes, the lighthouse is now both an aid to navigation and a tourist asset. Visitors' donations help to pay for its upkeep.

RIGHT *The restored Rose Blanche Lighthouse on the Southwest coast of Newfoundland, ready for its final coat of paint.*

BOTTOM LEFT *Work begins to stabilize the ruin.*

BOTTOM RIGHT *Work progresses.*

BOTTOM MIDDLE *The optic waiting to be installed.*

THE REST OF THE WORLD

So far we have looked mainly at the North American attitude to lighthouse preservation, but the work done here is being mirrored throughout the world. The lighthouse authorities in many countries are developing strategies to turn their lighthouses to alternative use. Some follow the U.S. Coast Guard approach; others are working in different ways. Britain's Trinity House has carried out an exhaustive survey of each lighthouse in what it calls its Lighthouse Estate. Each lighthouse was evaluated to determine its potential for alternative use that could be complementary to its prime role as an aid to navigation, and to establish its historic, architectural, and ecological value. The aim was to work in partnership with other agencies to utilize redundant dwelling as holiday homes or, where there was sufficient public access, to open selected stations as a visitor centers, the revenue this would raise would be used to maintain the historic structures.

So far, 12 out of 72 operational lighthouse are open on a regular basis as visitor centers, with further schemes being developed.

Although Trinity House no longer employs lighthouse keepers, each station has a part-time attendant who looks after the lighthouse and also works with whichever agency is looking after the conversion to alternative use, in partnership with Trinity House. Portland Bill is a typical visitor center where this scheme is in operation. The lighthouse here has stood on the tip of Portland Bill, a peninsular jutting out into the English Channel, since 1906, when it replaced an earlier lighthouse on a nearby site. In 1996 the present lighthouse was automated, and all the keepers left the station except one, Peter Fitch, who was given the job of part-time attendant. Trinity House retained the ownership of the tower, but sold the keepers' dwellings to the owners of the surrounding land, the Crown Estates. They, in conjunction with the local Weymouth and Portland Borough Council, now operate the converted dwellings as an center that is visited by 20,000 people each year. They can also visit the tower, where Peter Fitch guides them up its 153 steps in his full-time role as the site

BELOW *Toriñan Lighthouse, Spain, defaced with graffiti.*

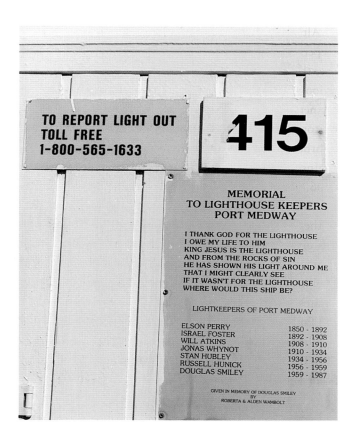

ABOVE *Port Medway lighthouse, Nova Scotia, is no longer manned or monitored. The Canadian Coast Guard relies on local people reporting if the light is extinguished.*

heritage custodian. This partnership provides a full time job for Peter Fitch, and ensures that both the operational light and the heritage building are kept in good order.

A MOVING STORY

As with all old buildings, the conservation of lighthouses is an ongoing program. Some eventually need major works, but none quite as drastic as that performed on two lighthouses that had to be moved to save them. The story of the moving of the lighthouse at Cape Hatteras is told in some detail (see page 184), but here we look at the move of Belle Tout Lighthouse in southeastern England, between Birling Gap and Beachy Head, which was in danger of falling 275 feet (84 meters) into the sea. It's a story not of an official organization or a preservation society working to save a historic building, but of a young couple, Mark and Louise Roberts, saving their own home. The lighthouse, built in 1828 on the chalk cliffs, was never successful, because it was often obscured from view by low clouds or fog. In 1902 Trinity House abandoned it, building a new lighthouse a mile to the east at the foot of the cliffs. The new light was lit on 2nd February, 1902, and the old lighthouse sold as a private residence. It had a varied existence under a number of owners, and one of its roles was that of providing

hospitality to King George V and Queen Mary in 1935, who were friends of Sir James Purves-Stewart, a distinguished neurologist who owned the lighthouse at one time. During World War II it was badly damaged and abandoned.

In 1996, the lighthouse was purchase by Mark and Louise Roberts. They were aware of cliff erosion, because the cliff in front of the lighthouse had eroded 55 feet (17 meters) back toward the structure since a measurement was made in 1835, which placed the lighthouse 107 feet (33 meters) from the edge. Calculations had shown that the structure would be in danger by the year 2100. Mark and Louise Roberts were undeterred, and refurbished the lighthouse as their family home. One night in November 1999, the owners were horrified to hear a massive rumbling. They left the lighthouse hurriedly and, looking back, they could see a huge dust pall hanging over their home.

Later, daylight inspection revealed that the cliff had fallen away. Only 10 feet (3 meters) was left between the tower and the drop into the sea. The work to move the lighthouse was

BELOW *Portland Bill Lighthouse, England. The present single tower replaced the old towers — the low light, which is now a bird observatory and field center, has retained its original appearance, but the high light lantern has been removed.*

now accelerated. A concrete raft was formed under the 850 ton structure, and it was moved along a track, away from the cliff edge, by computer-controlled jacks.

LOST AND FOUND

Lighthouse buildings are being saved all over the world, but just as important are the artifacts and items of everyday life on a lighthouse station. Many of these items were discarded, as in the case of the eclipser unit below, to be found and restored. Others were lost forever. Some, luckily for posterity, found their way into public and private collections in all types of museums. Some items are shown as part of a general display, such as the Chance brothers' optical equipment in the U.K.'s Science Museum, London. Some, particularly in recent years, have been gathered together in specialized lighthouse museums.

The Trinity House Lighthouse Museum at Penzance, Cornwall, in the southwest of England, is an example of how the conversion of a redundant buoy shed at the Penzance depot has been turned into a lighthouse interpretive center. Visitors, whether vacationers or lighthouse enthusiasts, can operate a variety of equipment, including a hand-powered foghorn. But the most popular attraction is a journey back in time to see a reconstruction of how the keepers lived and worked on the famous Eddystone Lighthouse. Museums at the Kinnaird Head lighthouse on the northeast coast of Scotland, at Dun Laoghaire in Ireland, the Shore Village Museum in Maine, and many others tell similar stories.

STATEN ISLAND MUSEUM SITE

In 1996, the president of the U.S. Lighthouse Society, Wayne Wheeler, set an initiative in motion to find a suitable site for a National Lighthouse Museum. Many possible sites were carefully investigated before the abandoned lighthouse depot at Staten Island, New York, was finally chosen. Though the site will need an estimated $20 million spent on it before the museum can open (2005 has been put forward as a possible date), it was felt that it was in the best location to ensure success. The depot, which has six major buildings and an extensive waterfront area, dates from 1864. It was in regular use as the central lighthouse depot until it was abandoned by the Coast Guard as a result of decentralization. The site is now owned by the city of New York, who contributed some of the costs ($11 million) toward the conversion of the site.

This chapter has shown a few examples of the present enlightened attitude to the preservation of heritage lighthouse. The International Association of Lighthouse Authorities (IALA), based in Paris, France, has been responsible for linking together the individual lighthouse-operating authorities of the world since 1957. The organization has recognized the importance of the lighthouse in heritage terms and is now working to assist members with advice on alternative use and conservation practice as well as creating specialist committees to ensure that the technical excellence in lighthouse technology is shared. It also sets internationally recognized standards for lighthouse operation. The IALA is not alone in the quest to maintain lighthouses: in 2001 a World Lighthouse Society was formed to link together lighthouse enthusiasts, preservation societies, heritage architects, and alternative-use operators to bring together a unique blend of expertise, so that lighthouses and their heritage are conserved for future generations.

TERRIBLE TILLY

I want to end this journey around some of the lighthouses of the world with an unusual story. We have shown some of the many alternative uses for lighthouse buildings. One that's hard to beat is the present use of the Tillamook Rock Lighthouse (see Chapter 4). The lighthouse served for 77 years, guiding ships from the treacherous headlands just south of the mouth of the Columbia. It was known by locals as "Terrible Tilly."

Over the years it became an integral part of the local maritime scene. It was decommissioned on September 1, 1957, when the last keeper, Ossie Oswald, called the lighthouse "a protector of life and property to all." The light was replaced by a 16-foot-high (5-meter) lighted whistle buoy with a radar reflector placed half a mile west of the rock. After the light was decommissioned, more than 400 individuals showed interested in buying it.

The light station was sold in August 1959 to a group of research contractors from Las Vegas. The difficult access made it hard to maintain, and the property suffered badly and was almost allowed to fall in ruin. Finally, in 1980, a Portland columbarium company rejoicing in the name Eternity at Sea bought the property (a columbarium is a place where urns containing the ashes of the dead are stored). The lighthouse was completely renovated and designated a National Historic Monument, and converted into a columbarium cemetery at sea, with annual interment. The rock was designated a federally protected wildlife refuge in 1994, home for thousands of sea birds, seals and sea lions.

RIGHT *The lighthouse at Mobile Bay, Sand Island, has been dark since being battered by hurricane winds and waves.*

INDEX OF LIGHTHOUSES AND LIGHT VESSELS